MW00780734

GENE

# Handbook Of

# JUDO

## A Step-by-Step Guide To Winning In Sport Judo

### *GLOSSARY AND INDEX INCLUDED*

**PRO-ACTION PUBLISHING**
A Division of Pro-Action Sports, Inc.
P.O. Box 26657
Los Angeles, CA 90026

# GENE LEBELL'S
# Handbook Of
# JUDO
## A Step-by-Step Guide To Winning In Sport Judo

### WITH MORE THAN 380 PHOTOGRAPHS

## ABOUT THE BOOK

This book is as valuable for the finalist as for the beginner. It is a summary of the favorite holds and throws of a national champion, organized by topic into a practical judo text. Written by national AAU judo champion. Gene LeBell presents an easy-to-follow text, illustrated with more than 380 photographs. Those techniques work best in actual competition include the many variations and special holds which Gene LeBell has learned along the tournament trail.

Step by step, the author unravels the intricacies of judo. They explain and illustrate falls, throwing techniques, escapes from hold downs, how to force the opponent on his back, chokes, strangling holds, armlocks, and locking the legs. They also discuss the development of a personal style, highlight the four ways to win and make suggestions regarding judo schools.

The popularity of sport judo is growing rapidly. It is a sport with rules of fair play, a prescribed costume, and frequent contests and tournaments. Each and every one of these elements is fully covered by Gene LeBell in a book written 'on the mat.' Mr. LeBell presents methods which lead to winning competitive judo and to adequate self defense.

## ABOUT THE AUTHOR

Gene LeBell is a holder of the coveted Black Belt (judo's highest award) and is well known in the field as an expert instructor. Gene LeBell operates his own judo school in Hollywood. "In fact," says Gene LeBell, "much of this book was written into tournament records, on gymnasium blackboards, and in student's notebooks over more than a dozen years of active competition and practice. Every single technique has been 'field tested' personally and proven successful." (Circa 1962)

Originally published under the title, *The Handbook of Judo: An Illustrated Step-by-Step Guide To Winning Sport Judo*. Republished by permission of Cornerstone Library edition through arrangement with Thomas Nelson & Sons.

Copyright ©1996 by Pro-Action Publishing. All rights reserved. No part of this book may be reproduced or transmitted in any form or by any means without the written permission from the Publisher. For information contact:

Pro-Action Publishing
A Division of Pro-Action Sports, Inc.
P.O. Box 26657, Los Angeles CA 90026.

Other books by Gene LeBell all from **Pro-Action Publishing**

- Grappling Master: Combat For Street Defense and Competition

- Gene LeBell's Grappling and Self-Defense For The Young Adult

- Gene LeBell's Handbook of Self-Defense

- Gene LeBell's Handbook of Judo: A Step-by-Step Guide to Winning in Sport Judo

Printed in the United States of America
ISBN # 0-9615126-6-0
Library of Congress Catalog Card Number 95-72481

# ACKNOWLEDGMENTS

We learned soon after conceiving the idea for this book that giving literary birth is a long and painful process, requiring the talents and energies of many devoted people. This book is the end result of more than our efforts alone. Werner Venetz was on the receiving end of just about every technique illustrated, Fuji Nazawa advised us in the preparation of the Glossary, and Miss Allen spent many hours in typing and retyping pages of manuscript. These are but three of the generous friends who have spent endless hours helping us, and it is to them and the many others who have assisted us, that we dedicate this book.

THE AUTHORS

Werner Venetz

Gene Le Bell

# FOREWORD

THIS is a book about sport judo, which is practiced, much as boxing, wrestling, and fencing are, in a gymnasium (or *dojo,* as it is known). Judo is just what the name implies, a sport with rules of fair play, a prescribed costume, and frequent contests and tournaments. For several years now it has been sanctioned by the AAU in this country and by similar amateur sports organizations throughout the world.

Sport judo is taught and practiced with the primary goal of developing proficiency in organized competition. All the techniques discussed in this book follow this basic pattern. However, as in the other "combative" sports, such as boxing, the methods are readily adaptable to self-defense.

Almost all sport judo practiced in the world today is conducted under methods, theories, nomenclature and techniques adopted by Dr. Jigoro Kano, who founded the Kodokan School in Tokyo late in the nineteenth century. For this reason, sport judo is often called Kodokan judo. Dr. Kano was to jujitsu what the Marquis of Queensbury was to fist-fighting.

Jujitsu is an older form of Japanese self-defense. It is still practiced throughout the world, and much of sport judo's techniques are drawn from it. There were, and still are, many other systems taught and practiced. Among these are *Tai-jitsu, Yawara, Aikido, Taido* and *Karate,* but few can be considered true sport; they are more accurately described as systems of unarmed combat.

It is not our desire to discuss the relative merits of these various systems, but merely to draw a distinction between sport judo and the many other systems which stress self-defense as their goal. Self-defense is not, specifically, a subject of this book, although much of this material is readily adaptable for this purpose.

We believe that both forms of the art, sport judo and self-defense, should be studied by the serious student. But self-defense is properly a separate subject, and space limitations prevent its being included in this book.

# Contents

        Ashi Waza
        (*Leg Throws*)

    Osoto Gari                               40
    Yama Arashi                              42
    Okuri Ashi Barai                         43
    De Ashi Barai                            45
    Harai Tsurikomi Ashi                     46
    Ushiro Ashi Barai                        47
    Hiza-Guruma                              49
    Ouchi Gari                               49
    Ko Soto Gari                             51
    Ko Uchi Gari                             52
        Variation                            53
    Uchi Mata                                54
        Variation                            55

                Tewaza                       58
            (*Hand Throws*)

    Tai Otoshi                               58
    Seoi Nage                                60
        Variation                            62
    Ippon Seoi Nage                          63
    Kata Guruma                              65

            Koshiwaza                        66
            (*Hip Throws*)

    Ogoshi                                   66
    Kubi Nage                                68
    Eri Tsurikomi Goshi                      69
    Sode Tsurikomi Goshi                     70
    Hane Goshi                               72
    Harai Goshi                              74

            Sutemiwaza                       75
        (*Sacrifice Throws*)

    Obi-Nage                                 75
    Tomoe Nage                               77
    Sumi Gaeshi                              78
    Kaniwaza                                 80
    Soto Makikomi                            81

CHAPTER 1

# FOUR WAYS TO WIN

MOST of the techniques of sport judo can be practiced by all age groups and both sexes. Not everyone, however, has the ability or desire to become an outstanding athlete, and for this reason, many students do not enter the contests and tournaments which are an essential part of sport judo to the student who wishes to win recognition and advancement in the form of trophies and higher belt ranks such as the coveted black belt, the symbol of the judo authority.

A student can become expert in sport judo only by entering into serious competition regularly. He must be in good physical condition, an athlete willing to train rigorously. Many students cannot, or do not desire to, meet these requirements. This doesn't mean that they cannot specialize in the study of self-defense, learning the rudiments of most of the sport judo methods as they apply to such problems as protection against boxing or wrestling, the disarming of an assailant, or the seizure and search or transporting a prisoner by police officers.

Judo in any of its forms is fun. It can be a rewarding, invigorating experience for young and old and for both sexes. The study of self-defense is an exciting and challenging exercise for mind and body. For the businessman who hasn't exercised regularly for years, for the young woman who wants to be able to protect herself in an emergency, for the physically weak, the small or the handicapped, or for the peace officer whose duties may expose him to danger of assault by prisoners or suspects, self-defense instruction by a competent judo coach fills a definite need.

Unfortunately, few schools in the United States offer instruction in both sport judo and self-defense. I believe that both should be taught and practiced in every judo school worthy of the name, because such a school is serving more people and doing a better job for its members. Judo has a great potential in this country, but it will be realized only through an ever-expanding membership of students in its gyms and schools. Restricting its benefits to relatively few outstanding athletes and old masters only tends to strangle its growth.

## On Choosing a Judo School

Both theory and practice are needed by the student of any sport. Few judo schools succeed in their efforts to balance these two elements properly. In some schools there is much formal instruction, lecturing and demonstration by the instructor and his assistants. Students are taught an endless variety of new techniques before they have mastered what has already been taught. It is one thing to understand the theory and principles, even the necessary procedure of a technique, and an entirely different thing to be able to execute the technique against an unwilling antagonist. The body's muscles and reflexes must be given time to adapt themselves to what the mind already understands. In sport judo, this needed practice is called *randori,* or "free exercise," and is actually informal, friendly competition among students with the aim being to improve each other's techniques rather than to win the upper hand over the partner.

Randori is to sport judo what sparring is to boxing. While some schools stress formal instruction at the expense of free exercise, the opposite is true in many others. In this latter sort of school, an old master serves as a sort of figurehead, while swarms of youngsters cover the mat nightly, eager to spend the evening in rough-and-tumble grappling. Here, very little formal instruction is presented. The class is called to order, roll is called, a few calisthenics are done together by the group, and then, at a signal, the mob scene starts.

Many years of practice are needed to learn much in the school that stresses randori and neglects formal instruction. Frequently, this school develops outstanding individual competitors, but a beginner seldom gets a good foundation in the sport within a reasonable period of time. Moreover, the beatings he must undergo in order to become an accomplished competitor frequently discourage him, so he may discontinue, another potentially valuable member lost to the sport.

The average American is accustomed to having any subject presented to him first in theory, then with the specific steps outlined in detail. Only then does the instructor have him put the instruction to actual test in the field, the lab, or the arena.

The moral is clear; a man can have the best boxing coach in the world teach him how to punch a bag, how to jab, weave and execute the proper footwork, but he will never become proficient in the sport until he has spent many hours in the ring actually boxing and sparring. Conversely, a novice boxer cannot become adept at the sport merely by slugging it out hour after hour, without competent instruction to go with his ring activity. To become a competent judoist, a student needs both instruction and practice; for without instruction he will practice his own mistakes over and over again; without adequate practice, his body won't be ready to execute much of what his mind has absorbed. Remember, when searching for the right judo school, look for one that regularly provides its students with a properly balanced diet of instruction and practice. A good rule of thumb, I believe, is to divide the evening evenly between the two.

## On Choosing a Style for Yourself

There is no one "correct" way to execute each judo technique. This is particularly true of the throws. The movements should be adapted to your own physique, temperament, and strategy. Until you have many months or even years of experience, however, it is wise to imitate, as best you can, the techniques as done by the expert whose physique most nearly approximates your own. Later, you may experiment with other ways of executing the maneuvers. If you find that a particular throw works best for you in an unorthodox manner, then by all means practice it that way, for it has become the "proper" way for you to do it. Many techniques described in this book are unorthodox variations of standard holds and throws. As you continue to learn and experiment and improvise, you will be developing your own style. Remember that if every judoist were to execute every move in an identical fashion, a lot of the fascination of the sport would be gone. The sport would cease to improve, and it would degenerate into a series of stylized exercises.

## Ways to Win

While in amateur wrestling there is only one way to win a match, namely to pin a man's shoulders to the mat, judo matches are won in four ways: (1) a properly executed, high throw, called *nagewaza*, dropping the opponent onto his back or side (2) an immobilization hold called an *osaekomi* in which a man is held under control on his back or side for a period of thirty seconds (3) a choke called *shimewaza*, directed against the blood vessels of the neck causing the opponent to lose consciousness or to submit (4) a joint lock, called *gyakuwaza*, directed against the elbow causing the opponent to submit to avoid a fractured arm.

The very fact that there are these four ways to win help make judo not only a fascinating participant sport but an exciting spectator sport as well.

Judo differs from amateur wrestling in many other ways. Every hold and technique available to the amateur wrestler is available to the judoist, but the wrestler is limited to holds which cannot injure or do not punish an opponent. There is no such limitation placed upon the judoist. The liberal rules of judo open up entirely new vistas to the student. In addition to the wrestling holds available against an opponent stripped to the waist, a judoist avails himself of his opponent's clothing, principally his jacket and belt, to provide leverage for scores of other techniques unique to his sport.

## NAGEWAZA

If either contestant is thrown from his standing position so that he strikes the mat on his back with appreciable force, the thrower is awarded a full point (*ippon*), providing the throw is made in good form (photo 1). If a throw is made which the referee doesn't consider sufficient to win the contest, but merits credit, he may award one-half a point (*wazari*). A match is won either by an ippon or two wazaris.

1

2

## OSAEKOMI

If a contestant is held on his back on the mat under complete control for thirty seconds, a point shall be scored and the match won. The technique of holding may be changed during the thirty seconds, providing the control is retained. If an osaekomi is held twenty-five seconds, but not thirty seconds, it shall count one-half point (photo 2).

## SHIMEWAZA

If a contestant is choked into unconsciousness or resigns the match to avoid the choke, a full point is secured and the match is won (photo 3).

## GYAKUWAZA

The match is won if a contestant acknowledges defeat when force is exerted so as to endanger the elbow joint (photo 4).

3                                              4

## Time Out

A bout may be stopped temporarily at the discretion of the referee when the contestants go off the mat, when a costume needs adjustment, or if he wishes to warn the contestants of rules infractions or to inspect an injury. If an osaekomi has been called and the contestants go off the mat, the referee may drag the two contestants to the center of the mat in their same position.

## Grappling Deadlock

If efforts toward securing any advantage while kneeling or recumbent become deadlocked, the referee may order the contestants to their feet.

## Illegal Holds

Unfair holds shall, if possible, be broken without discontinuing the bout, with the offending contestant being warned. If the illegal hold is repeated, the match may be awarded to the opponent.

The following holds are illegal: scissor holds on the head, throat or body for punishment; lifting and dashing a reclining opponent onto his back; placing hands or feet on the face; twisting fingers; hooking the foot in the opponent's costume or belt; tackling except as a counter to an attempted trip; full nelson; toe holds; hammer lock; locking other than the elbow joint; dragging the opponent into ground judo without attempting a definite technique; falling on one's back when an opponent is clinging there; inserting the fingers at the ends of the opponent's sleeve or trouser leg; binding an opponent's body with the belt or jacket; any hold which may injure the opponent's vertebrae.

## Stalling

Stalling is illegal. After two warnings, the referee shall award the match to the offended contestant, as a full-point win.

## Rankings in Judo

Beginners in the sport wear white belts. After proving their ability in contests against other wearers of the white belt, and after mastering fundamentals, students are awarded a brown belt. This usually takes about six months to a year. There are three degrees of brown belt to be earned in tournaments by defeating contestants of other schools of equal rank, consistently.

After three more years of regular practice and a successful record in many tournaments, plus a demonstrated theoretical knowledge of the myriad of techniques in judo, a contestant may be allowed to enter a special promotional tournament. If he defeats several opponents in succession, all of equal rank and experience, he is awarded the coveted black belt, the symbol of the judo authority. There are ten degrees of black belt from the lowest, *shodan* (first-degree black belt) on through *judan* (tenth-degree black belt).

| | | |
|---|---|---|
| Gokyu | 5th Class | White Belt |
| Yonkyu | 4th Class | |
| Sankyu | 3rd Class | Brown Belt |
| Nikyu | 2nd Class | |
| Ikkyu | 1st Class | |
| Shodan | 1st Grade | Black Belt |
| Nidan | 2nd Grade | |
| Sandan | 3rd Grade | |
| Yondan | 4th Grade | |
| Godan | 5th Grade | |
| Rokudan | 6th Grade | |
| Shichidan | 7th Grade | |
| Hachidan | 8th Grade | |
| Kyudan | 9th Grade | |
| Judan | 10th Grade | |

# CHAPTER 2

# THE FIRST FALLS

WHEN a student enrolls in a judo school, he first learns to fall safely. He is taught a system of special tumbling tricks, called ukemi, not common to any other sport. He must master these before he may compete because without a thorough knowledge of these tumbling methods he would quickly be injured by the violent throws practiced in the sport. Next, the instructor usually demonstrates the more common throws and holds used in the sport and watches the student practice the moves with a partner who co-operates. Then the new student is matched against the other beginners, and he is launched on his judo career.

## Ukemi

Many students find these falling techniques the most difficult part of judo. You may do falling exercises along with, or in place of, calisthenics for warming up before judo practice.

## Break-Fall Theory

Every one of us is born with a fear of falling. This fear makes the beginner tense and awkward when first learning to fall. He should remember five basic principles at all times. These principles apply to every fall he will take in his judo career.

1. Relax. Tense muscle transmits shock to the spinal column and this makes the fall painful. Relaxed muscle absorbs the shock. If a beginner is falling in proper position and yet is experiencing headaches or backaches, it is usually because he is falling stiffly with his muscles tense.
2. Don't reach for the mat. This is the most common cause of injury when falling. By reaching for the mat when falling to your rear, your hand supports the full weight and force of your falling body. This will frequently result in injury to the wrist, elbow or shoulder joints.
3. Avoid touching the mat with the spine, skull and all bony surfaces.
4. Spread the shock evenly over fleshy muscular surfaces of the body.
5. Slap.

A judo practice session or class usually lasts an hour or two. In that period of time the judo student will fall or be thrown scores of times. In order to fall painlessly and comfortably, the new judoist must learn to slap the mat violently with a limp arm just a split second before his upper body makes contact with the mat.

If you are going to fall on your left side, you would slap with your left arm. At the beginning of your fall your left arm should be extended to your right across your body much as though you were holding a baseball bat and getting ready to hit a right-handed home run.

5                                        6

7

8

9

10

As you fall, your arm whips across your body and strikes the mat violently. Your arm must remain limp. Allow your hand to bounce away from the mat immediately after contact. The arm should slap the mat at approximately a forty-five-degree-angle to the body. If you slap the mat with your arm too close to your body, you will be likely to roll up onto your arm, and thus expose your shoulder to injury. If you slap too far away from your body, you will be exposing your rib cage and the force of the fall will probably knock your breath out of you.

Photo 8 illustrates how you should land when falling to the left rear. You are slightly on your left side. Your right shoulder and right hip are off the ground. Your right knee is bent and is pointing straight up. Your left knee is flat on the ground. Your left ankle, knee and hip are touching the mat. Your left arm has slapped the mat, palm down. Your right arm is close to your body protecting your ribs. Your chin is resting on your chest so your head will not hit the mat.

Take a close look at photo 8, then switch from your left side to your right side, slapping with your right hand, putting your left knee up in the air and your right knee flat on the mat, having your left hand across your chest to protect your ribs, still having your chin on your chest.

After you have rolled from side to side, slapping with alternate hands many times, advance to photo 5.

From a sitting position, raise your left arm forward and across your body. As you fall, keep your chin in and look toward your left side. This will raise your left shoulder slightly. Slap the mat hard as you fall, keeping your arm limp and your body relaxed, letting your hand bounce. Your hand hits the mat slightly before your body so as to absorb much of the shock. Practice photos 5 and 8 many times until your teacher says you are ready to advance to a higher fall. When this is accomplished, advance to photo 6. Raising your weight on your right leg, straighten out your left leg and fall toward your left side, slapping the mat violently with your left hand. Fall as in photo 8. When you can do this without jarring yourself, advance to photo 7.

Stand up straight. Sweep your left foot in front of you until it gets so high that you have to fall as in photo 7. Hit the mat as in photo 8. This is the most common fall you take. Learn it well on both sides.

## Two-Hand Slap from a Sitting Position

Put your arms in front of you as in photo 9. As you start to roll backward, place your chin on your chest. As you fall, strike the mat with your forearms and hands slightly before your shoulders hit. This will eliminate much of the shock.

## Tumbling Forward from a Kneeling Position

Place your body in the same position as in photo 11. Your right knee is bent. The fingers of your right hand are pointed between your legs. Your right elbow should be pointed in front of you. You make a wheel out of your right hand, shoulders and hips. Look at your belt. This will lower your head. Do not roll on your head.

11

12

13

14

Stay off joints such as elbow and shoulder. Roll across these so no one part will have to support your entire weight. Kick off with your right foot (as in photo 12). Duck your head, roll and fall as in photo 8. When you have mastered this, both sides, advance to the standing roll in photos 13 and 14.

15

16

Step forward with your right foot. Your right hand should be in front of you starting the wheel discussed for the previous fall. Keep your chin tucked in and roll. Do not support your full weight on your hand when you fall. Your right hand is nothing more than a guide. Roll on your right arm, past your right shoulder, on to your left side and slap the mat violently with your left hand. Land as in photo 8. Note the wheel action in photo 14. Do this many times both sides. Then advance to photos 15 and 16.

## No-Hand Fall

This is called a no-hand fall because your right or guide hand does not touch the mat. From a standing position, swing your right hand between your legs. Springing off strongly with your right foot, swing your left foot back and up swiftly. Note that your left arm is cocked to slap hard when you are halfway over as in photo 16. Slap with your left arm violently just before your upper body hits. Land as in photo 8.

## Jumping Horse

A judo man eventually should be able to jump his own height. Get a little running room. If you slap with your left hand, take off on your right foot. On your way over, roll, slap, cross your legs and after landing, roll up into a standing position. Note: The palms of your hands touch the mat first. Make your body like a large hoop so no one part will support your full weight at any time. Eventually try to see how high and how far you can jump. See photos 17 and 18.

17                                    18

## Face Fall

Resting your weight on your knees, straighten out, falling forward. Slap with your forearms. Tilt your head back. The run-and-jump face fall as in photo 20 is interesting to try. Run and jump, arching your back, raising your arms in front of you at a slight angle. When you hit the mat, your arms should strike slightly before your body strikes. Try to land flat. If you hit too high on your chest, rolling forward, you may injure your spine.

19

20

21

22

## Handstand Into Side Fall

Kick off into a handstand as in photo 21. As you start to go over, turn your body so that you take a side fall as in photo 22. Do this on both sides.

**23**

**24**

**25**

**26**

**27**

**28**

## No-Touch Two-Arm Slap

Run and jump over an imaginary figure as in photo 23. Tuck your knees in close to your stomach. On your way over, begin to straighten your knees as in photo 24. Also note in photo 24 the position of your hands in anticipation of the slap. Hit the mat as in photo 25. Hands strike first. Your shoulders and the balls of your feet strike simultaneously.

From a standing position, bend your knees, bending your arms at your wait. Jump back and up. Swing your arms forward and slightly across your body as in photo 27. Hit the mat, striking both hands first. Your shoulders and back should hit simultaneously as in photo 28. Note: In this jump-back fall, your hips do not help break the fall.

## Off-Balance Principles

When a man stands erect with his weight evenly distributed on both feet, it is relatively easy for him to resist either a strong push or pull when that effort is made in a direct line with an imaginary line drawn between his ankles. In figure A, (page 31) you will note

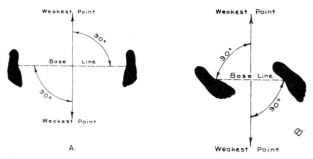

that this imaginary line is called the base line. If, however, the effort, either a push or a pull, is directed toward a point at a ninety-degree angle to this base line it is impossible for the man to retain balance unless he moves his feet. These weak points, front and rear, are illustrated in photos 29 and 30.

29                                              30

It is important to note that it makes no difference which direction the man is facing or his toes are pointing. The base line depends upon the relative position of the two ankles, independent of direction. Figure B (page 31) illustrates this principle. Photo 33 illustrates the off-balance principle presented in figure B. Although the toes are pointing "due south," the weakest points are diagonal to the direction his toes are pointing, which is actually a ninety-degree angle from the base line. This principle of off balance is applicable only when a man's weight is evenly distributed on both feet, usually when he is standing still.

When, however, he is shifting his weight from side to side, as in walking, a different principle called "point balance" or off-balance-in-motion goes into play. When a man has his weight balanced directly over one foot, a push or pull directly away from the opposite foot will be the effort he will find most difficult to resist. Remember that the push or pull is made directly away from the foot not bearing the weight. Remember also this direction is not dependent upon the direction his toes are pointing or the direction his upper body is facing. As in figures A and B, the base line is drawn independently of the toes or the upper body. Two of these "point balances" or off-balance-in-motion positions are illustrated in photos 31 and 32.

31　　　　　　　　　　　　　　32

33 34

Naturally, if a man has his center of gravity balanced over one foot, he can be tilted in any direction as in photo 34. His balance is most completely disturbed, however, when you push directly away from the nonsupporting foot because he will have to move his free foot the greatest possible distance before he is able to put it to the mat again and regain his balance.

## The Pivots

Although the execution of every throw in judo requires some shifting of a man's weight and balance, those throws known as *koshinage* or hip-style have a definite similarity of pivot. There are about a dozen basic koshinage or hip-style throws which make use of almost identical pivoting techniques. The choice of pivot is primarily up to the individual judoist. However, some throws are more readily adapted to one particular type of pivot and a judoist must learn through experience which of the basic pivots is most suitable to his own style.

## Forward Pivot

Face your opponent squarely at normal distance and in a normal stance. Your feet are about two feet apart. Assuming this is to be

35                36

a right-sided pivot, pick up your left foot and place it in front of and about six inches away from the toe of his left foot as in figure 1. Now shift your weight to your left foot with the toes pointing to your left and pick up your right foot, swing it around the front of your left foot and put it down again. Your back will now be to your opponent. See figure 2. You will note that figure 2 illustrates the spinning of the pivotal foot, the left foot, so that upon completion of the pivot both of your feet will be pointing directly forward. In this pivot, as in the other two which we will discuss, your weight should be shifted heavily onto your left foot at the conclusion of the pivot. By having your weight well centered on your left foot, you will be able to use your right leg freely in attacking the inside or outside of his right leg. You will note that in photo 36 the thrower's right foot has not been placed to the mat but rather is pressing on the outside of his opponent's right leg. In order to do this he has had to keep his weight centered over his left foot. For the completion of this throw he will not place his foot back on the mat until after his opponent has been thrown over the top of that extended leg.


## Reverse Pivot

Face your opponent squarely at normal distance with your feet about two feet apart. Pick up your right foot and place it on the

# FORWARD PIVOT

1.

2.

# REVERSE PIVOT

3.

4.

mat in front of and about six inches way from his right foot. Pick your left leg up and swing it around behind your right foot and place it on the mat shifting your weight to your left leg as soon as it touches the mat. Your back will be to your opponent. You will note that in figure 4 your right foot spins on the ball of the foot

37                                              38

to bring both feet around until they are pointing directly to your front. Photos 37 and 38 correspond roughly to figures 3 and 4. You will note again the thrower's weight is well-balanced over his left leg upon completion of the pivot.

## Skip Pivot

This is a difficult pivot to describe without actual face-to-face demonstration. Although the other pivots, the forward pivot and the reverse pivot, can be described in a series of definite steps, the skip pivot when properly executed is a blur of motion difficult to break down by the numbers. However, its basic motion is very similar to the reverse pivot.

Face your opponent at normal distance squarely with your feet about two feet apart. Pick up your right foot and very gingerly place the toes of your right foot directly between your opponent's legs and slightly in front of his toes. Now, for the sake of the pivot, pretend that you have a very tender area on the ball of the foot, or pretend that you are stepping on a tack, and while limping on

that right foot, as in photo 39, swing your left foot past the rear of your right heel and shift all of your weight onto your left foot as in photo 40.

## Moving-Wheel Theory

Every judo throw has some sort of circular motion either in the pivot, the leverage action, or the off-balance effort. Figure 5 illustrates one such motion during *seoi nage,* the shoulder throw. When executing this or any other throw, it is essential that your body move in smooth, fluid harmony. Straight, jerky action will defeat your purpose. Figure 6 shows the wrong way to move into position for seoi nage. The thrower has bent his knees at point **B** and turned his back to his opponent, but has hesitated momentarily there before straightening his legs to lift his man off his feet, which should have happened when his shoulders approached point **C**. By hesitating, and by moving in straight lines, he has not only lost the momentum of his pivot, but his body hasn't maintained tight contact with his opponent's. Consequently, his opponent's feet haven't yet left the ground in figure 6, and the attempt to throw will fail. In other words, by moving in straight lines, jerkily, from A to B to C, momentum and bodily contact has to be established three times instead of just once, as is illustrated in figure 5.

In figure 5, the thrower's shoulders act much like the rim of a wheel, with the hub of that wheel at his hips. The wheel spins

Correct
5

Incorrect
6

from A to B as he pivots, and from B to C and back to A as he completes the throw, in one continuous, circular effort. There was no hesitation at point A or B or C. The thrower didn't picture the throw in separate stages. He didn't think of going from A to B to get down low and then from B to C to raise his opponent on his toes and then from C to A again to finish.

In competition, the thrower is usually countered at one of these "corners"—A, B or C. If he rounds these "corners" at full speed, he is much less likely to be stopped short, his contact with his opponent will be maintained, and his over-all effort will be much more efficient.

A student learns each new throw in three separate stages. First, the instructor outlines it for him "by the numbers," showing him where his feet are to be pivoted, where his hands should be pulling, where his body is to be placed in relation to his opponent's, and in which direction he should pull and bend to complete the throw. Once he has learned the crude mechanics of the throw, he must then learn to mold the many movements into one united, flowing effort, with his entire body working in harmony. He does this in the second stage, which the Japanese call *uchikomi,* similar to shadow boxing for a boxer. At almost full speed, the student moves in and out of position for the throw fifty or a hundred times without stopping—like repeating a calisthenic exercise over and over again. In this way, the student learns to "round the corners" as in figure 5, and to eliminate all hesitation or jerkiness. Finally, he puts the throw to use in randori (free practice) during informal competition, many times, before using it in *shiai,* or tournament.

Practice these three stages with an opponent and you will find it will help you with all of your standing throws.

# CHAPTER 3

# THROWING TECHNIQUES

## ASHI WAZA
### (Leg Throws)

### *Osoto Gari—Major Outer Reaping Throw*

ASSUME natural position as in photo 41. Step forward and to the left with your left foot to a point about six inches outside and slightly to the front of your opponent's right foot. Shift all of your weight to your left foot. Pull his right sleeve forward and into your abdomen and push up and to your left with your right hand, tilting him as in photo 42. Swing your right foot forward and around behind his right leg and whip upward and backward with your right leg as in photos 43 and 44. Your swinging leg, the right leg, should not touch the mat until he has landed, as in photo 45. The back of your thigh should strike the back of his thigh and your entire leg should swing between his legs.

Note: Your right arm should flex tightly against your right shoulder for maximum strength and leverage. Be sure your balance is distributed well forward and your body is hunched forward as you step into the throwing position. The best moment to execute this throw is when your opponent's weight is supported on his right heel.

41

42

43

44

45

## Yama Arashi—Variation of Osoto Gari

When executing this throw, you will be at a considerably greater distance from your opponent than you were when executing osoto gari. Pull strongly on his right sleeve and step to your left with your left foot as in photo 46. Bend well forward at the waist and shift all of your weight to your left foot which now should be about eighteen inches diagonally forward and to the right of his right foot. The calf and Achilles' tendon of your right leg strikes the rear of his right knee. Continue pulling his right sleeve forward and to your left and whip backward and upward with your right leg against the rear of his right knee. Meanwhile your right arm shifts from its normal position. Clenching your fist, press your ulna bone against his right shoulder and continue the pressure while your forearm slides down against his biceps toward his elbow as in photos 47 and 48.

Note: This throw requires a strong, twisting, pulling, tilting action of your arms against your opponent's right arm and shoulder to put him in a very weak off-balance position before your leg executes the throw.

Note: In this throw, as in osoto gari, your right leg, the swinging leg, does not touch the mat again until your opponent lands on his back. This throw is useful against an opponent who is stiff-arming you and circling you counterclockwise.

46

47

48                                              49

## Okuri Ashi Barai—Double-Foot Sweep or Pursuit-Foot Sweep

Assume normal position. Your opponent side-steps rapidly to his left. Follow his side-stepping and get in step with him. As he shifts his weight to his left leg and begins to slide his right leg toward his left, as in photos 50 and 51, your weight should be on your right foot. Lift your left leg, curl the toes and rotate the foot inward, placing the sole of the foot against the outside of his right foot just below the ankle bone. Your sweeping foot should slide across the mat as it approaches his right foot. The sole of your

50                                              51

sweeping left foot pushes against the outside of his right foot and directs it against his left ankle as in photo 52. Meanwhile your arms are lifting his lapel and sleeve upward in a rotating, counterclockwise action. This action of the arms is first directed to your right in order to settle his weight well on to his left leg. Then pull upward to raise his body on to his toes as the sweeping action is commenced as in photo 52.

**52**

Continue the lifting action while pulling him tightly against your chest. Keep your stomach well forward and your head up so that you do not bend forward at all from the waist. Arch your back and extend your sweeping leg diagonally forward and past the front of your right leg. When your opponent's legs are leaving the ground, the left side of your body from left ankle to left shoulder should be in a straight line as in photo 52.

Note: The toes of your supporting right foot should point directly to your opponent's left. In other words, your right foot points in the direction you intend to sweep his feet, as in photo 50. To complete the throw, continue to pull upward and to your left as you sweep forward and to your right with your left foot, as in photo 53. Your left leg should continue to sweep almost until your opponent lands on his back.

53

54

## De Ashi Barai—Lower-Foot Sweep or Single-Foot Sweep

This throw depends entirely upon split-second timing for proper execution. Your opponent is advancing with his right foot. At the instant before his right foot completes its step, immediately before it touches the mat, curl the toes of your left foot and flick the sole of your foot rapidly against the outside of his right foot below the ankle bone. Push his right foot to his left (your right) and pull him forward and to his right (your left) as in photo 56. In this throw, as in okuri ashi barai, be sure that you do not bend forward from the waist. Arch your back and lean to your left rear, the direction in which you are pulling your opponent.

55

56

## Harai Tsurikomi Ashi—Lifting-Ankle Sweep

Your opponent is retreating and in doing so, steps back with his left foot as in photo 57. His weight is on his right foot. Step forward rapidly with your left foot just to the outside of his right leg and shift all of your weight onto your left foot, extending your right leg and curling the toes of your right foot until the sole is against his left shin, as in photo 58.

Now, as you lift with your arms against his sleeve and lapel, shift your entire body's direction to the right, twisting your opponent to your right. Continue to push with your right foot as you pull him upward, around and down to your right. Once you have made contact against his left shin with your right foot as in photo 58, you shift your body in the direction your arms are pulling to tilt him to his left front. In order to regain his balance he would have to place his left foot back on the mat. But because you have pressure on his left shin with your right foot, he is unable to move that leg and consequently, falls to his left front or your right rear. Be sure to pull him tightly against your body as you step into position in order to obtain maximum leverage.

57                                      58

**59**

## Ushiro Ashi Barai—Rear-Foot Sweep

This throw differs from the other foot sweeps in that the opponent's weight is on the foot you are sweeping. Its successful execution depends to a major degree upon the proper use of your right arm to direct his left upper arm against the left front of his face and forehead. Pull him so he steps forward with his right foot as in photo 60. At this point, your weight should be on your right foot. Place the sole of your left foot, toes curled, against the heel of his right foot as in photo 62. Meanwhile lift his left arm by pushing upward against the sleeve at his left elbow. Continue this lift until his upper arm is pushed tightly against the left side of his face and forehead as in photo 61. Push with your left hand against the outside of his right elbow so that his right elbow is pushed inward against the front of his abdomen as in photo 63. These three movements—the foot, the right arm, and the left arm —are executed simultaneously. The throw is completed by continuing the pressure upward and inward against the left side of his face, and by pulling and lifting with your left foot against his heel as in photo 64.

Note: This is a dangerous throw and it is easy to land a man high on the back of his neck, so be careful when executing it.

60

61

62

63

64

## Hiza-Guruma—Knee-Wheel Throw

If executed properly, this throw should give your opponent the same feeling as he would have if he were being pulled and twisted over a small fence, knee-high. Holding in a natural position, take a large step to your opponent's left side with your right foot, pointing your right toes towards his right ankle. At the same time, lower his right shoulder by pulling his right sleeve downward with your left hand and raising his left shoulder with your right hand as in photo 65. Also, place your left foot just above your opponent's right knee. Continue to twist your body from right to left. Keep your left arm and elbow close to your side. Throw by continuing the arm pressure on his upper body as in photo 66. Keep your left foot just above your opponent's right knee as long as possible. Land him safely as in photo 67. Be careful not to injure your opponent by jamming your foot violently against his knee. You are not striking his knee with your foot; you are placing it.

65                              66                             67

## Ouchi Gari—Major Inside Reaping Throw or Inside Leg Hook

The ideal time to execute this throw is when your opponent's legs are spread wide apart in a pulling, defensive posture. Pull down with your left arm, straight down between his toes and make a sideward motion with your right arm, pulling him around to his

68                              69

left or your right. It will get your opponent to take a large step
with his left foot. His right foot should be firmly in place. Thus
your opponent has his feet wide apart. Naturally, the wider his
feet are apart, the easier it is for you to put your right foot in and
hook his left leg. If your opponent's legs are wide apart, he can
not shift his balance easily from one leg to the other.

When you are ready to attack, pull your opponent close to you
and hook at the same time. Your right calf should hook behind his
left knee just below the knee joint as in photo 69. Pull your shoulders as close as possible to his shoulders so you will be like one
moving mass. When you attack, your bodies will be locked together
as in photo 70. As your right leg is lifting his left leg off the ground,
apply a strong push to his left rear corner and lean heavily in that
direction, throwing him on his back. If you keep close to your
opponent while he is falling, as in photo 70, he will not be able
to turn or squirm away. He should land flat on his back as in
photo 71.

70                              71

## Ko Soto Gari—Minor Outer Reaping Throw or Outside Leg Hook

This technique is a good contesting throw. You will find it even better as a countertechnique. When your opponent comes close to you either in attacking, or by your pulling him, then is the time to attack. Reap your right leg around your opponent's left leg with as little wasted motion as possible, as in photo 72. Hook your opponent's leg securely behind the knee. Hold his leg securely with your leg on his way down so he may not turn or get away.

72

73

Note in photos 73, 74 and 75 how your right leg never lets go until your opponent's shoulders have come in contact with the mat. Pull your opponent's chest as close as possible to your own so you will be locked together. Make a lunge forward. Swing your right leg back as in photo 74, as though you were doing uchi mata, inside thigh sweep, but keep your leg bent or hooked around his leg while doing so. Driving forward, try to throw your right knee higher than your belt or waist, keeping in mind that the object of this technique is to force both your opponent's shoulders to the mat at the same time, as in photo 75.

74

75

## Ko Uchi Gari—Minor Inside Reaping Throw or Inside-of-Leg Sweep

The easiest time to attack with this technique is when your opponent's legs are far apart and he is trying to pull away from you, with his weight more on his heels than on the balls of his feet. Pull his right arm to your left, counterclockwise. This should make him start to take a large step with his right foot as in photo 77. Keep your left foot in place. Pull his right sleeve with your left hand close to your stomach.

76

77

Just before he puts his full weight on his right foot, sweep inside the heel of his right foot with the sole of your right foot. Strike the heel low and in the direction his toes are pointing. Simultaneously, pull your opponent's right arm close to your body, leaning forward and pushing with your right arm so that your opponent will be forced to put his weight on the foot that you are sweeping.

It is important that the sole of your foot maintains control of your opponent's right foot at all times so that his leg cannot escape. If you sweep his foot just before he puts his full weight on it, he will have the sensation of slipping on a banana peel.

Drive him to the mat as in photo 78. Lean heavily forward and to your left, and with your right hand, palm downward, push towards an imaginary spot on the ground over his right shoulder. Your opponent does not fall straight back, but diagonally toward his right hip and side.

78                                79

## Ko Uchi Gari—Variation of Minor Inside Reaping Throw or Inside Leg Hook

Pull your opponent toward you with a downward motion. Your opponent resists by spreading his feet and leaning backward. If you give a good pull, he will have to bend his knees quite a bit to resist. At this time, your feet will be at least three feet away from him. Drive with your right arm, trying to strike with the point of your right shoulder against your opponent's right armpit as in photo 80. At the same time, hook your right leg around your op-

80                              81

ponent's right leg well below the knee. With your right hand, grab his right pant leg and drive toward his right rear and roll from right to left as in photo 81.

If you find your technique is going to be successful, you may break your fall by putting your right palm on the ground just before you hit. Another way to break your fall is to keep winding on the way down and fall with your complete weight on your opponent's stomach, but be careful because your opponent will take a rather hard fall when he catches your entire weight. As soon as you have come in contact with the mat, make a rapid turn and face your opponent. This will minimize the chance of getting choked from behind.


## Uchi Mata—Inside Thigh Sweep

Uchi mata, although often confused with a hip-style throw, is a leg throw. It is the inside of your thigh, not your hip, that hoists your opponent off the ground. Uchi mata is a good technique to try when your opponent is in a defensive position. Break your opponent's balance by pulling him strongly forward. When your opponent braces, as in photo 82, put your right foot forward in a skip pivot. Pull him onto your back, turning forward, as in photo 83, skipping to your other leg. Your thigh is as deep between his legs

82 83 84

as possible. Pull with your left arm close around your chest, making your opponent lean toward his right shoulder. With your right arm, pull your opponent on your side as close up to your neck as possible. Twist your body to the left with as much momentum as possible. Swing your right leg as though it were a pendulum high off the ground; at the same time, lower your head and turn it to the left. Raise your left heel off the ground for extra height as in photo 84.

A very important factor in the success of this throw is having your opponent snug against your body as high up as possible. The back of your right thigh should slide up the inside of his left thigh to his lower abdomen.

Note: In photo 83 your left knee is bent. When making the throw, you straighten your knee and raise on your toes for extra height as in photo 84. Remember to bend down so that you are able to get in deep.

## Uchi Mata—Variation of Inside Thigh Sweep

This technique is done with a forward pivot. This is a very fancy way of doing uchi mata and is effective for many judoists; however, many believe the skip-pivot uchi mata is a more effective throw and

85

86

87

88

89

90

much harder to counter. A good time to attack with this technique is when your opponent is circling to his right (your left). Make a forward pivot with your left foot leaning slightly backward to enable you to keep your opponent going in his original direction by applying circular pull with both hands as if you were swinging a rope and he were on the other end. He would have to take large steps whereas your steps could be small.

Note in photo 85, your opponent's weight is on his left foot. Because of the steady pull with your left hand toward your chest in a circular motion, when you are ready to complete your throw as in photo 88, your opponent's weight is evenly distributed on both feet. Pull your opponent in as close as possible. Notice in photos 87 and 88 how the attacker's shoulders turn counterclockwise and the head begins to lower. If you have your opponent close to you, it is your body that is furnishing the momentum, and not your arms. In continuation of this move, swing your right foot as high to your rear as possible, raising his feet off the ground as in photo 89. Hold your opponent close while he is in the air as in photo 90 so you have full control of his body and may land him safely.

In the other uchi mata where you skip in, you hold your opponent's sleeve with the left hand and his collar with your right hand. He is generally confident from the position of your hand that you are going to attempt a right-sided throw. But in spinning your forward-pivot uchi mata, you hold both lapels at the armpit. This enables you to attack to the right or left with equal ease. In this book, the techniques are demonstrated from one side only. Without making the throw, practice uchikomi, or repetition of this technique, on both sides, pivoting in and getting your opponent off balance, at least one hundred times every evening. Fifty times right side and fifty times left side and you will be astounded at how quickly you will be able to master this.

# TEWAZA
## (Hand Throws)
### Tai Otoshi—Ankle Block

This is just one of the many ways to attack with this throw which works exceptionally well on a short, stocky opponent. A good feature of this technique is that it is very difficult for your opponent to achieve a clean counter throw on you. Note in photo 91, the attacker's hands are pointing out his opponent's full step. If done properly, the opponent never achieves a full step.

Jam the ball of your right foot onto the mat, heel up, as in photo 92, forcing his foot onto the mat in the middle of his forward step. Thus, your opponent is still leaning forward and in an off-balance position. Simultaneously, pull with your left hand in a downward, circular motion as in photo 93. You throw your right hand straight out as though you were throwing a boxer's right cross with your fist. As your opponent starts to go over, pull sharply downward with your left hand close to your body and raise your right knee as in photo 94. Keep your left arm as close to your chest as possible and pull with your left shoulder muscle.

91                                    92

In throwing the simulated punch with your right hand, place your right elbow as close to your hip as possible for better leverage. In the start of your swing, keep the fist of your right hand as close to your own right shoulder as possible.

93

94

95

Before attempting this technique, point your body towards your opponent's right shoulder. This will actually eliminate a pivot. All you have to do is quickly place your right foot in starting position as in photo 92. You may get your opponent in position by pulling him around with your left arm to make him take a large step with his right foot. Or, push your opponent backward violently. He will eventually force his way forward, taking a large step, giving you the same chance. When your opponent starts his journey through the air, he should be on the ball of his right foot, and leaning extremely forward. His knee will be bent forward. His right shin will be leaning against your right ankle and calf. Raise your right knee as in photo 94, and it will help your opponent's right foot leave the ground and aid your own technique in completing the throw.

## Seoi Nage—Cross Lapel Throw

In competition you should not have to fight for one particular grip. If your opponent is smart, he will not let you have the grip you are fighting for, so learn to attack from many different hand holds. There are many different hand positions for various forms of Seoi Nage. This particular grip is good because you hold both lapels evenly about armpit height as in photo 1. This enables you to attack either right or left with equal ease. In a normal contest position, you will have one of your arms under one of your opponent's and the other arm over his other arm. He will, of course, be in the same position. If his left arm is over your right arm, you spin in right-sided. If his right arm is over your left arm, you spin in left-sided.

In this particular movement, the attacker is doing a reverse pivot, beginning the throw when the opponent moves forward, helped by a slight pull. When he takes a step with his right foot, place your right foot in position as in photo 96. When he makes his following step with his left foot, you should be turned into position as in photo 97. Spin in fast, coming in with your legs bent. Your belt should be below his belt. Slam into your opponent violently. As you are straightening up, you will find this helps get your opponent off balance. Lift and turn with your right shoulder. Your left hand should be pulling his lapel snug against your body. Turn to the left, counterclockwise. Straighten your legs and bend forward. Most of your weight should be on your left foot, as in photo 98. Your right foot, with just the ball of the foot touching the ground, should be used for balance. This enables you to raise your hip to advantage.

Note in photo 97 the crossing of the hands. Your left hand is in front of your right wrist. Your wrist is as close to your right shoulder as possible. As the man starts to go over, roll your right shoulder forward, pulling down and to your left with your left hand.

96

97

98

99

Concentrate on moving your arms, body and legs simultaneously for maximum effect. Force your head down and to the left as in photo 97. You will note that your shoulders follow this motion.

## Seoi Nage—Variation of Cross-Lapel Throw

This technique looks similar to Tai Otoshi although you are in quite a bit deeper for this one. The best time to start this throw is when your opponent is circling to your left, moving toward you but still not too close to your body. Holding in a natural position, pull down and toward you with your left hand. Turning your body, push with your right arm and turn his shoulders as in photo 100.

Note: You will find that if you keep your arms close to your sides, your body is getting your opponent off balance as much as your arms. This movement will jam your opponent's right foot into the ground. Spin in fast as in photo 100. Note that your opponent has taken a step bringing his right foot forward as in photo 101. The inside of your right thigh is preventing his right foot from moving or taking another step. Note, also, in photo 101 the position of your hands. Your opponent's armpit is resting on your right arm between your elbow and wrist. Pull downward hard with your left hand so this position cannot be changed.

100                                      101

To complete this technique, pull with your left arm close to your body in a downward right-to-left motion. Move your right shoulder to the left in a circular motion as if you were taking a forward roll as in photo 102. At the same time, you should be straightening your left leg, raising your body. Straighten your right leg, raising your right hip, and push your right shoulder forward as in photo 102. Hold on to your opponent's right sleeve to break his fall as in photo 103.

102

103

## Ippon Seoi Nage—One-Arm Shoulder Throw

Probably the most common pivot used in this throw is the reverse pivot. Your left hand is on your opponent's right lapel. Your right hand is on your opponent's left sleeve as in photo 104. Pull with your right arm, keeping your elbow close to your body. Turn your shoulders clockwise. Chances are, if the man has never worked with you before, that he will think you are attempting an osoto gari and in an attempt to counter will lean his right side forward. This means that he will be on his toes leaning forward.

Using a steady strong pull with your right arm as in photo 105, start your pivot. Double up your left fist. As you begin your pivot,

104

105

throw your left fist, arm and shoulder toward your opponent's left armpit. Drive your arm and shoulder upward and around in a circular motion as if you were taking a left-handed rolling fall. Retain a strong pull with your right arm in a downward motion and a tight grip with your left arm around your opponent's tricep. This should immobilize the left side of his body.

Note in photo 106 your weight is primarily resting on your right foot. Your left foot is on the ground only for balance and to help you raise your left hip in the air as you follow through with your technique.

Sometimes you will find that your opponent is not far enough up on your back to complete this technique. Then, bend your knees lower and work backward rapidly, using quite a bit of pull with your right hand and push with your left shoulder. These steps must be short and very fast. To complete this, raise your hips by straightening your legs. You will note that your opponent's feet begin to leave the ground as in photo 106. Continue pulling with your right arm and raise your left shoulder and left arm, using your back muscles, and continue to straighten your legs.

106

107

## Kata Guruma—Shoulder Wheel

The straighter your opponent stands, the easier it is to get into position for this throw. Bending down, take a long right step between your opponent's legs. At the same time, pull strongly with your left hand against his right sleeve as in photo 108. Hit your shoulder hard into your opponent's right thigh and right hip. Pull

108

109

110

111

him close. Squat and shift his weight from your right shoulder to your left shoulder as you are straightening your legs. Throw your opponent to your left front. Notice the position of the shoulders in photos 108, 109, and 110. Your shoulders are like the steering wheel of an automobile turning from right to left in a circular motion. Remember: Squat more than you stoop for the greatest leverage.

# KOSHIWAZA
## (Hip Throws)

### Ogoshi—Major Hip Throw

Assume natural position. Pull your opponent's right sleeve with your left arm, keeping your elbow close to your waist. Bend his right shoulder slightly toward the mat. Take a reverse pivot, stepping in with your right foot first and then your left. Your hips should be well below his belt. Your weight should be on your left foot. As you are moving in, place your right arm around your opponent's back. Pull him snug to your body as in photo 112. Straighten out your left leg, raising your right hip. The effort should be in your left thigh when throwing your opponent, as in photo 113. As he goes over, release your right arm, but continue holding his right sleeve with your left hand to break his fall.

**112**

**113**

**114**

## Kubi Nage—Head-Lock Throw

The pivot of this throw, from the hips down, is much the same as Ogoshi. Start your reverse pivot, placing your right foot forward. Put your right arm around your opponent's neck. Pull his right sleeve with your left hand while keeping your elbow close to your waist. Bend slightly forward as in photo 116. Then complete your pivot by placing your left foot into position and securing your right arm tightly around his neck. Hit into this throw hard with your hips. Pull your opponent's neck forward and down with your right arm. Pull his right sleeve downward, to the left, in a rotating

115

116

117

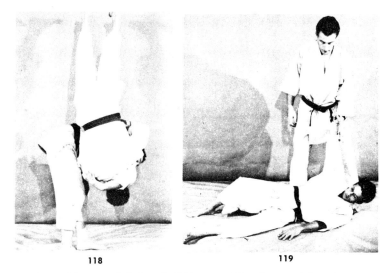

118   119

motion with your left hand. Lift your hips by straightening your left leg. Throw as in photo 118. Let go with your right arm and continue to hold on with only your left hand to break your opponent's fall as in photo 119.

## Eri Tsurikomi Goshi—Lifting-Lapel Hip Throw

Like Ogoshi, in this throw you do a reverse pivot, stepping first with your right foot. Pull your opponent close to you. Do this by pulling his right arm with your left hand counterclockwise and pulling his collar close to you with your right hand as in photo 120. Then, as in photo 121, you pivot on your left foot. Raise your

120

121

right arm, hoisting your opponent on his toes. Straighten your legs by raising your right hip. Keep a steady pull with your left hand and push with your right to insure control of your opponent's body while he is in the air.

122

123                                                              124

## Sode Tsurikomi Goshi—Lifting-Sleeve Hip Throw

Although a reverse pivot is more common, I prefer and use here a forward pivot. This throw is effective when an opponent pushes you or straight-arms you as in photo 125. Help your opponent straighten his left arm by pulling with your right arm close to

125

127

126

your body in a clockwise circular motion. Then, keeping your elbow close to your hip, begin to raise his arm as in photo 126, if your opponent's arm is fully extended, it will be at its weakest point. Start your forward pivot, still attempting with your right arm to put his left arm over your right shoulder as in photo 127.

With your left hand, pull your opponent's right lapel close to your body as in photo 128. Keep your left elbow in close to your body. Hold a tight grip and rotate your body in a counterclockwise motion. Throw your right shoulder and arm out hard as if you were trying to throw a heavy iron weight for distance. When your opponent is halfway over, drive your right arm, which is still holding his left sleeve, down toward the mat as in photo 129. If desired, you may hold the man's left sleeve until he hits the mat. This will give him little chance to escape while he is in the air and no chance to slap the mat to break his fall.

Note: The thrower puts his foot in a tai otoshi position. If he reaches his right foot way out, it will enable his left foot to get deeper into the hip style throw. Then, when making the throw, he raises his left knee as he turns his body counterclockwise.

128                                        129

## Hane Goshi—Bent-Knee or Spring-Hip Throw

The ideal time to attack with this throw is when your opponent is moving toward you. Two of the more common ways to hold the jacket while attempting hane goshi are: 1) holding your opponent's right sleeve with your left hand and your right hand on his left lapel under his armpit; 2) holding both lapels at the armpits. If your opponent forces both of his arms under both of your arms, you may still do this throw right or left.

Start your skip pivot pulling and lifting your opponent well onto your right hip and side as in photo 131. Bend your right knee slightly and place it in front of your opponent's right foot as in photo 132. The throw is done with the side of your body and your hip. Your right leg guides your opponent over. Keep your opponent close to you and high on your chest while completing this throw. If you are fortunate enough to grip underneath your opponent's arms and he is straight-arming you, bend your arms as you pull your opponent toward you. His arms will be on the outside of yours and he will be forced to bend his elbows.

130

131

132

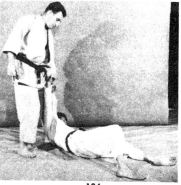

133

134

## Harai Goshi—Outside Thigh Sweep

Although a reverse pivot is demonstrated here, a forward pivot could be used. Start your opponent moving forward forcing most of his weight on to his right toes. Do this by pulling downward on his right lapel with your left hand. Keep your left elbow close to your body. Push with your right arm against his left lapel at armpit height as in photo 135. Pivot in, using strong arm motion. Place your right leg and your right calf below your opponent's knee, but

135

136

do not touch the mat with your right foot until after the throw is completed. Continue your throw by lifting and sweeping with your right thigh high in the air. For extra lift, you should be on your left toe at the height of this technique. Complete the throw and land your opponent safely.

# SUTEMIWAZA
## (Sacrifice Throws)

137

138

## Obi-Nage—Belt Throw

This is not a popular throwing technique, but it is a good move to get your opponent on the ground for mat work. Place your left hand around the back of your opponent's neck on his collar. Your right hand should be on his belt. Swing your right foot up to gain momentum. Kick it hard from right to left pulling downward

139

140

strongly with your left hand as though you were going to take a
high fall. As your opponent is three quarters of the way down,
your right arm should begin to push at his stomach as though he
were taking a Tomoe Nage fall. Keep your left hand close to your
body at all times as in photo 142.

In attempting this, do not let your right hand leave your opponent's belt until the throw is completed. If you miss the technique
and fall on your back and your opponent is over you, you can get
your knees into his stomach quickly and easily if you already have
a secure hold on his belt. When you get as far as photo 143, roll
up into a side pin.

141

142

143

## Tomoe Nage—Circle Throw or Somersault Throw

Hold your opponent in a natural contest position. Push him backward until he resists your push. Jump at once, placing your left foot at his appendix. Keep your left knee bent and shove your right foot in between his legs as far as possible as in photo 146.

144

145

146

You land on your back. Your belt should be between his legs. Keeping your left foot on your opponent's abdomen, raise it up and toward your head. At the same time, pull your arms toward your sides and make his shoulders come close to yours. His hips will now be higher than his shoulders. When the throw is completed as in photo 148, turn your body over quickly and secure control of his body on the mat.

147                                      148

## Sumi Gaeshi—Corner Throw

With your left hand on your opponent's right sleeve, pull with a downward right-to-left motion until his weight is on his right foot. Jump off the ground placing your right foot below his left knee and keep your left leg straight. His right ankle should touch your left calf and Achilles' tendon. As you fall toward the ground, keep a tight hold as in photo 150. This will force your opponent to bend over. Continue to pull strongly with your left arm in a downward motion so the point of his right shoulder will be forced toward the mat as in photo 151. At the same time, straighten and lift with your right foot below his knee to complete the throw.

Note: The back of your left ankle hits violently against your opponent's right ankle. When the throw is completed, continue to roll until you are on top or have control of your opponent.

149

150

151

152

153

## Kaniwaza—Flying Scissors

Your opponent is pulling away from you with his left side far
forward as in photo 154. Pull with your right hand strongly toward
your body. Jump in a scissoring motion as in photo 155. Twist your
body from right to left. Swing your right leg across his stomach
and push with your left leg above the knees. Land your opponent
on his shoulders.

This is a beautiful throw when executed properly although I
do not recommend it for competition because it leaves you in a
precarious position when you hit the mat.

154

155

156

## Soto Makikomi—Winding Throw

This technique looks like a hip-style throw. The difference is that in a regular hip-style throw, you toss your opponent over your hips or back, but protect his fall by holding his sleeve so that he doesn't land on his head or shoulders. In a Makikomi throw, you throw the man over your hips or back but try to wind until you land on top of your opponent as in photo 160. This doesn't give him a great deal of protection in landing.

Grab your opponent in a normal position. Take a forward pivot or skip pivot with your left foot between his legs as far back as possible. At the same time, pull with your left hand on your opponent's right sleeve, turning your back toward him. Let go with your right hand, forcing it between his arms and over his right shoulder as in photo 157. Start your opponent's journey through the air by raising your right hip and right leg, at the same time lowering your head and right shoulder, winding your shoulders from right to left, equivalent to taking a forward rolling fall as in photo 158. I do this with the aid of what looks like a Hane Goshi, raising my right knee, which helps in this technique. Thus you may call this throw, Hane Makikomi.

157

158

Note: You are still pulling and keeping your opponent's right arm close to your chest by pulling steadily with your left hand against your opponent's right sleeve. Continue to wind your body as in photo 159. Raise your left heel off the ground for extra height. Continue your forward winding motion until your opponent hits the mat as in photo 160. Note the position you are in. Most of your weight is on your opponent's chest. You may do this another way: you may touch your right hand to the mat and let your opponent roll off your hips, thus protecting his fall, although it will not be nearly as effective in competition.

159                          160

# CHAPTER 4

# TURNING THE TABLES

YOU have been on the offensive. Now you must learn some countering techniques. Defense, of course, is all important and the best defense, as in war, is a powerful counter-attack.

## *Block to Uchi Mata—Used for Hip-Style Throws*

As your opponent moves for his technique, bend your left knee, hitting strongly forward with your left hip, throwing your right shoulder back and raising your right foot off the ground for balance as in photo 161.

161

83

## Block to Ippon Seoi Nage—One-Arm
## Shoulder Throw Counter

As your opponent begins his attack, bend your legs and hit your opponent's right hip with your left hand in a downward motion.

Note: If he drops to his knees, you may choke him from behind.

162                                    163

## Block to Harai Goshi—Outside Thigh
## Sweep Counter

As your opponent turns his back to you, bend your right knee, dashing your left calf in front of your opponent's left leg below his knee. Pull strongly with your right arm against his left lapel and push back strongly against his left foot.

Note: In photo 163, if you bend your right knee enough, his right foot will hit much too high on your right thigh to make this throw successful.

## Utsuri Goshi—Switching-Hip Counter Throw

As your opponent starts to move in for a hip-style throw, bend your knees and grab the rear of his belt with your left hand and with your right hand maintain your grip on his left lapel, as in photo 165. Lift your opponent by bending your arms, bumping him forward with your stomach, and pulling him close to your chest, straightening your legs and standing on your toes for extra height, as in photo 166. Switch your weight onto your right foot, bending your left knee and rolling your hip forward toward his lower body. Swing your opponent's body backward on his way down as in photo 167 so that the front of his abdomen will hit your left hip as in photo 168. As he is resting on your left hip, as in photo 168, do a left-handed Hane Goshi or bent-knee throw by continuing to raise your left hip and leg. Your opponent should land on his back, slapping with his right arm.

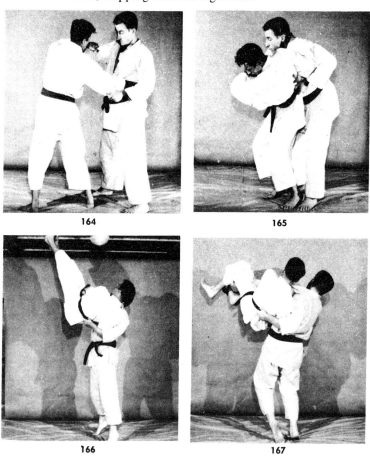

164

165

166

167

168

169

## Ura Nage—Back-Drop Counter Throw

This throw is particularly good if you want to get your opponent on the mat for ground work. As your opponent turns his back to you for any reason, push down and forward against his right elbow with your left hand, pulling backward with your right hand against his left lapel as in photo 170. At the same time, begin to bend your right knee, swinging your left foot behind his left calf. As he begins to bend his knees, start pulling his right sleeve down and backward, turning your body counterclockwise to face your opponent as in photo 171. Your left Achilles' tendon strikes hard below your opponent's left calf to lift his feet off the ground. Face him and drive his shoulders into the mat as in photo 172.

## Uchi Mata—Counter to Ko Soto Gari

As your opponent begins to hook your right leg with his left, turn hard to your left on the ball of your left foot, as in photo 174. At the same time, pull your opponent's right sleeve with your left hand, keeping your elbow close to your waist. Place your right hand around your opponent's neck or on the collar. The inside of your right thigh will already be on the inside of his left thigh. Swing your right leg high into the air, lowering your head, twisting his body so his back will hit the mat.

170

171

172

173

174

## De Ashi Barai As a Counter to De Ashi Barai

As in photo 175, your opponent begins to sweep with his left foot. He should be pulling down on your right sleeve, lowering his left shoulder. This will eventually help you as you bend your right knee as in photo 176, making a quick counterclockwise circular movement from your knee down, striking his left ankle with the sole of your right foot, as in photo 177. Continue the downward movement of his left shoulder by pulling his left lapel to his left and down. Lift his right arm with your left hand as though you were turning the steering wheel of an automobile and direct him onto his back.

175

176

177

## Ko Soto Gari—Counter to Harai Tsurikomi Ashi

Your opponent is leaning back when he attempts harai tsurikomi ashi—"lifting ankle sweep." He is pulling you forward. Bend your right knee, wrapping your lower leg around his left knee, hooking it as in photo 179. Hold your opponent close to you. Drive forward. This forward motion should not be difficult because your opponent is already leaning backward. Keep your body close to your opponent on the journey down so he will have little chance to turn away.

178

179

## Leg Lift—Into Ouchi Gari

This is an ideal counter to attempt when your opponent attacks with his left foot high off the ground as in photo 180. Grab his ankle with your right hand, pull it close to your body as in photos 181 and 182.

At the same time, hook your left calf behind his right knee. Sweep it forward as in photo 182. With your left hand on your opponent's right lapel, push toward his left rear.

## Grapevine and Choke—Counter to Seoi Nage

As your opponent turns his back to you, pull his left collar strongly with your right hand as in photo 183. At the same time, with your left foot, hook and grapevine his left leg as in photo 184.

180

181

182

183

184

185

Then place your left hand on his left collar high up. Lean to your left rear. Let go with your right hand, bringing it around behind his head and grabbing the left side of his judo suit as in photo 185. Apply a scissoring motion with your forearms, choking your opponent.

Note: Do not bend your wrists when choking your opponent. You may push your opponent onto his face or lie down on your back and do a double grapevine while choking him.

## Heel Sweep—Counter to Ouchi Gari

When your opponent starts his throw, shift onto your right foot as in photo 186. With your left hand pull your opponent's right sleeve toward your left side and down, straightening your body. Your right hand should be pushing your opponent's left lapel in an effort to turn your opponent sideways as in photo 187. At the

186

187

same time, strike the sole of your left foot against your opponent's left Achilles' tendon. Sweep and lift with your left foot. Pull and turn his upper body and throw toward your left or away from his left leg as in photo 188. Land your opponent safely.

188                                    189

## Thigh Lift—Counter to a Head Lock

As your opponent grabs you around your neck, move your hips away from his. Reach behind and between his legs with your right hand; your left hand around the front of his left thigh. Join your hands and lift his right leg off the ground as in photo 191, setting him onto his back.

190                                    191

### Block to Tomoe Nage

As your opponent attempts this throw, as in photo 192, slap your left forearm against his right ankle, pushing hard from left to right. Push his right leg past your body to your right so that his right foot misses your body entirely. He will be on his back and you will be ready for ground work.

192                                          193

### Stocks As Counter to Kata Guruma

Your opponent is reaching between your legs with his right arm and is pulling your right sleeve with his left arm. His head is against your right thigh. Shoot both your legs far to the rear. Jam your

194                                          195

left forearm in front of his left arm between your body and his, then bend your arm and put your left hand on his back. Your right arm winds around his neck and you lever upward against his right shoulder and arm with your left arm as you twist downward against his neck with your right arm, forcing him to fall on his back as in photo 195.

Note: This technique is effective against most kinds of tackles or leg dives.

# CHAPTER 5

# WINNING ON THE MAT
## (Grappling Techniques)

GRAPPLING techniques are not as common as standing techniques in judo competition, although they are of equal importance. A good judo man must be able to work as well on the ground as when standing. In competition, grappling techniques are used when one or both of the opponents fall to the mat, usually after an unsuccessful throwing attempt.

There are three legal ways to win a match on the ground with grappling techniques:

*Oeaekomi—Immobilization Holds*
   You must hold your opponent on his back for a period of thirty seconds and have complete control of his body.
*Shimewaza—Strangling Holds*
   Strangle your opponent by applying pressure against the blood vessels on the sides of his neck (not against the larynx) until he surrenders or becomes unconscious.
*Gyakuwaza—Arm Lock Techniques*
   Apply pressure against the elbow joint of your opponent making him surrender because of acute pain. In judo competition, locks against the elbow joint are allowed; all other joint locks are considered too dangerous although you may practice the locks in the regular workouts.

## Mat-Work Defense

Photo 196—If you are on the mat, and not already on your back, quickly roll to that position. Face your opponent and rotate your feet toward him as in photo 1.

Photo 197—If your opponent moves toward you in an attempt to do ground work, place your feet against his legs, holding him at bay. Place your elbows against the insides of your knees, protecting your rib cage against your opponent's attempt to get around or over your legs onto your upper body.

196                                         197

## Countering Leg Defense

### SINGLE-LEG GRAB

Quickly grab your opponent's right ankle with your hands. Straighten his leg by pulling it past your right side as in photo 196. When your opponent's leg is straight, he is unable to defend his right side, so quickly come in on this weak side with ground-work grappling techniques. Photo 199 shows the start.

### DOUBLE-LEG GRAB

Grab your opponent's pant legs as low as possible, one in each hand. If his pant legs slip above his knees, grab an ankle in each hand and start the same technique as in photo 200. Swing his legs back and forth, from left to right, confusing him. Then, quickly

**198**                    **199**

**200**                    **201**

throw his legs out to your right, shoving your right knee against your opponent's right thigh, as in photo 201, knocking out his defense. Attack on his right, weak side for ground-work grappling techniques.

## MAT WORK ADVANTAGE OR DISADVANTAGE

In wrestling, if you rest your weight on your back, pinning your shoulders, you lose the match. This is not so in judo. Thus a judo participant may attack by resting his weight on the mat, using the mat for a wall to push his opponent away with his feet, or aiding the control of his opponent's body with his feet as in photo 202. In photo 202 you (the bottom man) have a decisive advantage over your opponent because you have your feet at his hips, controlling his body. This makes it very difficult for your opponent to come toward you in an attempt to choke or pin.

Photo 203—The bottom man is at a disadvantage. In this photo, as you can readily see, you (the bottom man) cannot push your opponent off with your feet because he is over your feet. He can choke you easily or do a smother pin and you have little choice in the matter. Remember one thing: in mat work use your feet as much as possible in controlling your opponent's body. Your feet are much stronger than your arms and a man who uses just his arms is using less than half of his body's potential.

202                              203

## The Triangle Theory

With your opponent on his back, imagine a triangle drawn on his upper body. His right shoulder being one angle, his left shoulder being the second angle and the middle of his waist below the tie of the belt, the third angle. As your opponent tries to get up by rolling to his right, raising his left shoulder off the ground, place your right forearm, elbow and the greater part of your weight on his left shoulder or second angle as in photo 204 until your opponent's shoulder touches the mat again. Do the same thing if your opponent raises his right shoulder or first angle, only use your left arm and side.

**204**                           **205**

If your opponent bridges his back, raising his hips off the ground, place most of your weight on his lower waist, or third angle, as in photo 205, until his hips touch the mat again. You can straighten his legs either by grapevining his legs or by pushing against his heels with the soles of your feet.

## The Outrigger Theory

### FIGURE 7—KUZURE KAMI SHIHO GATAME—MODIFIED UPPER FOUR CORNER HOLD AND SMOTHER

Note your feet are close together. There is no outrigger effect. You and your opponent are like two boards as figured below. There is nothing stopping you from being rolled over on to your back.

### FIGURE 8—MODIFIED UPPER FOUR CORNER HOLD AND SMOTHER

The same technique except your feet are spread far apart forming an outrigger. Note the difference between the board in figure 2 and the board in figure 1. With the outrigger, as in figure 2, the board or the two bodies are more difficult to roll.

### FIGURE 9—KESA GATAME—SCARF HOLD

Note your body forms a 90-degree angle to that of your opponent, forming an outrigger, making it very difficult for your opponent to roll. Refer to the next chapter for the correct form on holding these techniques.

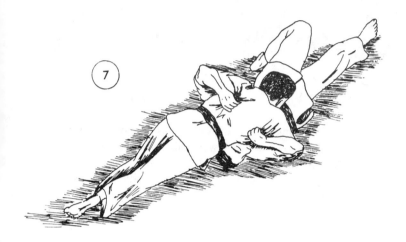

When your feet are together, you are in a
weak position and easily rolled.

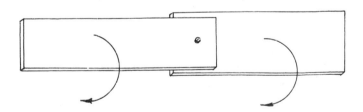

When your feet are spread apart, you
are in a strong position and difficult
to roll.

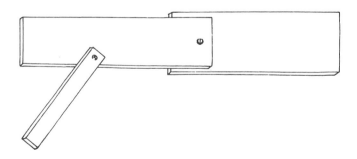

If your body forms a 90° angle to that of your opponet you are in a strong position and difficult to roll.

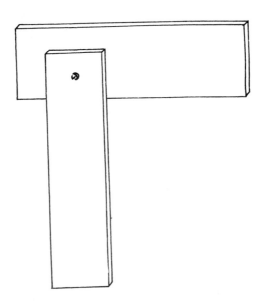

# CHAPTER 6

# OSAEKOMIWAZA— HOLD ON THERE!

## Hold Down Techniques

### KESA GATAME: SCARF HOLD

THROW your opponent so that he has to slap the mat with his left hand. You are still holding on to his right sleeve with your left hand. Fall into position, sitting alongside your opponent with the right side of your body resting on his chest. Put your right arm around his neck. Place your right hand on the mat as in photo 206, or grasp your pant leg with your right hand, or grab your opponent's collar behind his neck with your right hand. You may put pressure on his ribs by pulling his right elbow close to the left side of your chest with your left hand, rolling your left shoulder backward.

Note: The complete right side of your right leg is resting on the mat but only the sole and heel of your left foot are touching the mat.

### KATA GATAME: SHOULDER HOLD AND CHOKE

You are on your hands and knees with your left hand pushing your opponent's right arm over his head. Slide your right arm around his neck. Grab your right hand with your left as you get into a sitting position. Slide the top side of your right wrist against your opponent's neck, cutting off the blood supply to his head.

206

207

Push your head against the outside of his right arm and his head. Continue to pull your left elbow snug into your body. You will now have a hold-down as well as a choke (photo 207).

208

209

## KUZURE KAMI SHIHO GATAME: MODIFIED UPPER
## FOUR-CORNER HOLD AND SMOTHER

With your opponent on his back (photo 208), place your upper chest on his chest. Place your right arm underneath your opponent's right arm and place your left arm over his left arm. Grab your right wrist with your left hand between your opponent's neck and the mat. Squeeze tight. Spread your legs. Raise your knees, and place most of your weight on his chest. You may find it will be more difficult for your opponent to escape if you rest part of your chest and stomach on his face, cutting most of his wind supply.

### KAMI SHIHO GATAME: UPPER FOUR-CORNER HOLD

With your opponent on his back, place your chest against his. Place both your arms over both of his arms, grasping his belt in your hands. Your knees may either be into his shoulders as in photo 209, or out in a tripod position as in photo 208, or flat against the mat spread apart. Pull your opponent's belt toward your waist rolling your shoulders and chest into his chest.

### KUZURE YOKO SHIHO GATAME: MODIFIED SIDE FOUR-CORNER HOLD

With your chest on your opponent's stomach and chest, place your right arm underneath his right leg, and your left arm between your opponent's right arm and neck and around his neck, grasping your right hand with your left. Bury your head deep into your opponent's left side. Place your right knee snug against his right side. Place your left foot straight out for stability (photo 210).

### MODIFIED FOUR-CORNER HOLD: OVERHEAD WITH NEAR LEG

Your opponent is on his back. You are trying for a modified upper four corner hold (photo 208) and your opponent tries to escape your attempted move by rolling into you. By this time you have your right arm under his neck. Quickly hook his left leg at the knee and grab your right hand with your left as in photo 211. You will find that any pin that has your opponent's neck bent either forward or to the side makes it more difficult for him to escape.

### MODIFIED UPPER FOUR-CORNER HOLD: OVERHEAD WITH FAR LEG

This hold down is similar to the last one except that you grab the far leg instead of the near leg. If your opponent is on his back and he tries to get away by rolling on his left side, with your right arm under his neck, quickly wrap your left arm around his right leg and grab your right hand with your left.

Note: In photos 211 and 212 the pushing motion with your feet enables most of your weight to rest on your opponent's chest.

210

211

212

213

## KUZURE TATE SHIHO GATAME: MODIFIED UPPER
### FOUR-CORNER HOLD

Your opponent is on his back and you are on top of him. First hook your legs on the inside of his legs spreading his legs apart as in photo 213 to make it more difficult for him to roll. Quickly scoot forward. Your left hand is holding your opponent's right arm close to your body. The right side of your head is pressing against the mat. Your right arm is around your opponent's neck. In other words, his head is between your arm and right side. Your right hand grabs either your opponent's judo suit at the armpit or your own belt.

214       215

### KUZURE TATE SHIHO GATAME: MODIFIED UPPER
### FOUR-CORNER HOLD AND SMOTHER

Lying on your opponent's body, grapevine his legs to gain control of his lower body (photo 214). Wrap your arms around the back of his neck pushing your opponent's face into your chest, cutting most of his air supply. If your opponent turns his head to his left, move your upper body to your right until his right ear is resting against your left shoulder. Then, pressing against the back of his neck, slide your upper chest from your right to your left side, forcing your opponent's head or face to turn straight forward into the middle of your chest, thereby smothering him.

### USHIRO KESA GATAME: BACKWARD SCARF HOLD

Get into a sitting position facing your opponent's belt (photo 215). Wrap his right arm around your waist holding it snug against your body with your right hand as if you were starting a reverse time hold, but instead of rearing back as in a reverse time hold, place the left side of your body over your opponent's upper chest and neck. Place your left arm underneath his left arm above the elbow. Grab his belt with your left hand, entangling his left forearm in his own belt.

### BODY RIDES

Here are three ways to hold a man down, none of which counts as a pin.

### KNEE RIDE

Although dangerous in competition, this hold down can be useful in practice (photo 216). With your hands, grab your opponent's lapels at his armpits; place your right knee in the middle of your opponent's chest. Pull upward with your arms, raising your opponent's upper body; press downward into his chest, pressing his ribs slightly in order to shorten his breathing or collapse his lungs. Keep your balance with your left foot. The right knee should not only press into his chest but should be free to move along his body, preventing him from moving any part of his body. Your hands control and prevent his body from twisting or turning.

### DOUBLE BAR ARM

With your opponent on his back, place your left foot over his left arm above the elbow. Scissor your left leg with your right. Wrap both your arms around your opponent's right arm above the elbow. Hold on tight. This is not counted as a legal osaekomi or pin, but it is very difficult for your opponent to get up (photo 217).

 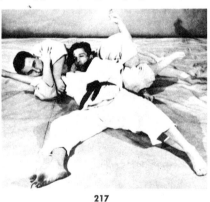

216                              217

### PIN DEFENSE

This is not an Osaekomi. If you are on the mat and find your opponent is superior to you on ground work and he is attempting to pin you, grab him around one knee with your arms. Duck your head and squeeze his leg at the knee. With your legs, drive forward pressing your left shoulder into your opponent's thighs and waist. From this position it is very difficult for him to get a pin, choke or lock (photo 218).

218

# CHAPTER 7

# DOWN BUT NOT OUT

### ESCAPE FROM KESA GATAME: SCARF HOLD

IF your opponent has you in Kesa Gatame (photo 219 Hold Down Techniques) and you have your arms around his waist, grab his belt. Push his belt away from your body to your upper right. Lift him at the waist. When his hips are off the ground, shove your right knee under his body as in photo 219. Pull your opponent close to your body at the belt while shifting him from your right to left side by a strong pull downward and to the left with your left

**219**

220                                           221

hand and push off strongly with your right foot as in photo 220. Keep on pulling until you are on your stomach and your opponent is on his back, as in photo 221. From this position, you may go into a hold down of your own.

### ESCAPE FROM KATA GATAME: SHOULDER HOLD
### ESCAPE INTO AN ARM LOCK

If your opponent has you in a shoulder hold and choke as in photo 222, begin your roll by placing your left hand on your left hip. Raise your legs straight up as far as possible as in photo 223. Place your feet over your left shoulder dropping on your knees in a backward somersault as in photo 224. When you get to your knees, you will find your opponent is face down and his right arm is nearly extended. Grab with both hands around his wrist and do a sit-out placing his upper arm underneath your armpit. Raise your hands and his wrist holding his shoulder down with the weight of your body. Keep your elbows in. This will put on pressure and lock his right arm as in photo 225.

### ESCAPE FROM KUZURE KAMI SHIHO GATAME: MODIFIED
### UPPER FOUR-CORNER HOLD

If your opponent has you in a modified upper four corner hold, straighten out your right arm and grab your opponent's right pant leg as in photo 226. Pull his leg down to your right side. Hook

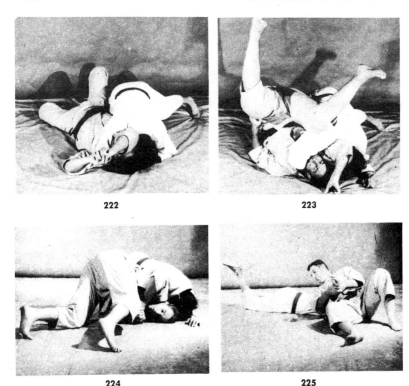

222                              223

224                              225

your right leg around his right leg as in photo 227. Grab your
opponent's belt by placing your left hand over his left shoulder.
Squeeze your opponent tightly, making it difficult for him to shift
his weight, as in photo 227. Pull his belt with your left hand shoving his head down and under with your left elbow. Place your right
hand on his stomach and push, rolling to your left, as in photo 228,
until you are on top of him and he is on his back.

### ESCAPE FROM KUZURE YOKO SHIHO GATAME—MODIFIED
### SIDE FOUR-CORNER HOLD

This is an odd but practical way of getting out of a side pin or
a wrestler's crotch and nelson. This is called a "figure 4 neck roll."
If your opponent has you in a side pin such as the one shown in

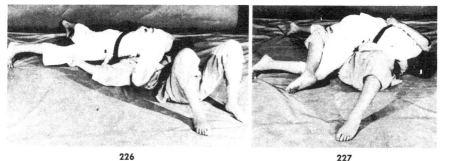

226          227

photo 223 in Hold Down Techniques, put your right leg over his head and snug against his neck as in photo 231. Then place your right leg over your left foot in a figure 4 position. Begin to roll your body at the shoulders as in photo 232. Still holding a snug grip with your legs, push with your right knee against his upper chest. Pull with your left knee against the back of his neck and head, bowing his head. Continue rolling until you are on your stomach as in photo 233. If desired, when your opponent is on his back, grab either his left leg or his left arm, holding the man securely in a pin as in photo 229.

228          229

230

231

232

233

234

In practice, if you want to have a little fun with your opponent on the ground, start your roll from photo 229. Continue through photo 234. You may roll your man over many times until he gets dizzy and at the end you will be in the position shown in photo 234. Sit up then on your right heel, putting pressure on your opponent's neck, making him submit.

## ESCAPE FROM SCHOOLBOY PIN

If your opponent sits on top of you, grabbing your wrists as in photo 235, straighten your arms over your head, grasping your hands, making his body move forward, and weakening his position as in photo 236. At the same time, wrap your right foot around your opponent's left ankle sliding your heel into his leg. Press off with your left foot rolling from left to right as in photo 237, until your opponent is on his back. His legs will still be around your waist. This is a good opportunity for you to go into a Boston Crab, as shown in photo 221, Leg Locks.

## ESCAPE USING SWITCH

This escape is not necessarily a pin escape but it is an escape when your opponent has semi-control of your body. You are on your knees and your opponent has his right arm over your right side and he may be starting an attempt for a winding choke. Before he gets his left hand on your right collar, start your switch by throwing your right arm back and over his. Kick your left leg in front of your right and scoot far out as in photo 239. Wrap your right arm around your opponent's right knee and thigh. Note where your right arm is in photo 239. From there you drop your right shoulder forcing your opponent on his face. Then quickly roll to the right, placing your left hand around his waist and pulling him close to your body. Then you are behind your opponent as in photo 240. When starting your go-behind, do your switch rhythmically and not in separate, distinct moves.

235

236

237

238

239

240

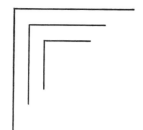

# CHAPTER 8

# WING LOCKS

### NEAR SIDE

YOUR opponent is behind you and you are on your knees. Wrap your right arm around his right arm well above his elbow. Pull his arm snug against your upper chest as in photo 241. Kick your right leg far out to your left front, throwing the back of your left shoulder against the front of his left shoulder as in photo 242. He lands on his back as in photo 243 with most of your weight on his chest. Then roll quickly on your stomach and knees, rolling to your left toward his legs and ending up in a hold down of your own as in photo 244.

241

242

243                                    244

### FAR FRONT

This is probably the most common of the wing locks. Grab your opponent's right arm with your left arm well above his elbow, pulling it close into your upper chest. Keep your right foot in place as in photo 245 and kick your left leg to your right side and front, throwing the back of your right shoulder against the front of your opponent's left shoulder, rolling him on his back. When your opponent's shoulders hit the mat, roll quickly to your hands and knees so that you are facing him.

### NEAR SHOULDER

If your opponent wraps his right arm around your neck in an attempt to strangle you, grab his right sleeve with both hands above his elbow (photo 246). Drive forward with your left foot rolling your right shoulder down, making your opponent take a forward roll onto his back. You should land on top of him and in an upper four-corner hold (photo 247, Hold Down Techniques).

### NEAR FRONT

You and your opponent are on hands and knees, facing each other, your head under his. Grab his right sleeve above the elbow with both hands, pulling his right elbow toward your belt on your right side. Straighten your right leg. Swing your left leg to your right side, throwing the back of your right shoulder against the front of your opponent's left shoulder forcing both of you to your backs. Roll quickly to your knees to secure a hold-down (photo 247).

245

246

247

# CHAPTER 9

# GETTING THE UPPER HAND— GRAPEVINES

### , GRAPEVINES

GRAPEVINES are used to control a man's lower body and are usually done in conjunction with other techniques. For example, if you do a winding choke, as in photo 249, the man cannot roll to either side.

### SINGLE-REAR GRAPEVINE

In photo 248, you may do a single-rear grapevine while you are doing a simple ride. (A "ride" is just putting your weight on your

248                                    249

opponent without a specified hold.) In photo 248 you have your opponent's left foot grapevined with your left and your right arm is wrapped around his right arm. If he is successful in rolling over, you are still clinging tightly to his back. Photo 249: Your right foot grapevines his right foot, stabilizing you while you lift his right wrist with your right hand, making your opponent fall on his face.

### DOUBLE-REAR GRAPEVINE

Wrap your legs around your opponent's waist and grapevine both of his legs, preventing him from rolling from side to side while you do the choke. Arch his back by arching your own.

### SINGLE-FRONT GRAPEVINE

Hook your right leg around your opponent's left thigh, grapevining. You may stop him from rolling to the side with this technique or you may put pressure on his left leg by straightening your right leg.

250          251

### DOUBLE-FRONT GRAPEVINE

Resting your weight on your opponent's stomach and chest, grapevine both of his legs as in photo 252. Lean forward and place your hands over his shoulders on the mat or, you may place the weight of your forward body on his shoulders, pinning them. Spread your opponent's legs slightly apart with your own. For pressure, straighten your legs as in photo 253. This locks his legs, which is illegal in competition.

252

253

## FRONT-GRAPEVINE ROLL

Pull your opponent on top of you. Place your right foot on the inside of his left thigh. Wrap your left leg around his right leg, placing your toes underneath your opponent's right ankle as in photo 254. Grab his sleeve at the right shoulder with your left hand and grab his left lapel with your right hand. Press your opponent's right knee into the mat with your left leg and begin to turn him by raising your right leg as in photo 255. Pull your opponent's right shoulder to the mat with your left hand. At the same time, with your right hand, raise your opponent's left shoulder and with the aid of your right shin on the inside of his left thigh continue to

254

255

roll your opponent on his back as in photo 256. When you are just about over and on top of him, pull your right leg out from in between his legs and place it on the outside of his left thigh.

Since rolling the shoulders over the mat, or "quick pins," do not count in judo mat work as in wrestling, a judo player has the opportunity to wrestle with his back on the mat, enabling him to use his feet to advantage.

Note: Keep in mind that your legs are much stronger than your arms. Do not be afraid to use them. For example, at times it is easier for you to push your opponent away with your legs than it would be with your arms.

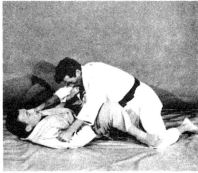

256                              257

## OUTSIDE LEG PUSH

Lying on your back, place both of your feet against your opponent's hips; at the same time, with a lapel in each hand, pull your opponent toward your shoulders and close to your chest as in photo 257. Then slide your right foot down your opponent's left thigh until it reaches his left knee. Keep your left knee bent and snug against his right hip. At the same time, straighten your right leg until your opponent's left leg is straight and he drops on his left side as in photo 258. Pull your right arm and your opponent's left shoulder close to your chest. Push his right shoulder away by straightening your left arm, rolling your opponent onto his back. Roll with him and on top of him, keeping your bodies close together. You should end up in a smother pin as in Hold Down Techniques.

258                                    259

Note: If desired, as you are rolling your opponent on his back, slip your hands from his lapels underneath his arms and touch your hands together behind his shoulders. Lean forward and begin to fold your arms, hugging his upper body. This will force your opponent's arms over his head making it more difficult for him to breathe or escape as in photo 259. Or you may do a conventional smother pin as in Hold Down Techniques.

## STOCKS AND CHANCERY

Start on hands and knees. Press your upper chest against your opponent's right shoulder blade. Place your right hand on your opponent's left arm, above the elbow. Place your left arm underneath his right arm and rest your right hand high on his back. Do not put your left elbow in too deep while your opponent still has his balance or you will be subject to near-front wing lock. Pull your right hand toward your belt straightening your opponent's left arm and forcing him on his left front side, as in photo 261. At the same time, press your left foot into the mat. Begin to straighten your left leg. Squeeze your opponent's right arm and shoulder close to your upper chest as his right side is raising off the ground. Keep driving until your opponent's right shoulder touches the mat and you fall diagonally across his chest.

## PIPE WRENCH

One good thing about a pipe wrench is that your opponent cannot attempt a wing lock. Starting on your knees, place your left

260

261

262

263

wrist behind your opponent's neck. Place your right arm underneath his body between his neck and right shoulder pressing your right hand on your left wrist. Pull yourself snug against your opponent's body as in photo 262. Press your right hand on your left wrist, downward, turning your left wrist inward, putting pressure on your opponent's neck. This will force his head and neck downward. At the same time, press and lift with your right shoulder against your opponent's left side as in photo 263. Snap him over and end up in a smother hold down.

### QUARTER-NELSON

Starting on your knees, place your left hand on the back of your opponent's neck. Place your right arm underneath his left shoulder and grasp your left wrist between your opponent's left shoulder and neck with your right hand. Straighten your left leg. Place your right shoulder snug against your opponent's left side as in photo 264. Your right hand pulls down on your left wrist, turning your left palm toward you. Put pressure on your opponent's neck forcing his head and neck downward. At the same time, your right forearm is raising your opponent's left shoulder and armpit as in photo 265. As your opponent is on his way over, drop your left knee to the mat and help him over with a push with your right shoulder as in photo 266. End up in a smother pin or in a reverse-time hold.

264

265

266

### NEAR HALF-NELSON WITH ARM DRAG

Place your left forearm under your opponent's left armpit, with the palm of your left hand on the back of his neck. Place your right hand on your opponent's right arm above the elbow. Place your right shoulder snug against the left side of your opponent's body. Place your left foot in pushing position as in photo 267. Pull his right arm close to your belt. Lift up under your opponent's left shoulder with your left hand pulling down against the back of his neck. Shove with your right shoulder until your opponent is on his back as in photo 268.

**267**　　　　　　　　　　**268**

### THREE-QUARTER NELSON

Starting on your knees, place your arms underneath your opponent and around the back of his neck as in photo 269. Place your right shoulder snug against his left side. Snap your opponent over by pulling your hands on the back of his neck close to your belt, driving your right shoulder forward. He will land on his back as in photo 270. You easily fall into a smother pin as in Hold Down Techniques.

### FULL-NELSON INTO PIN

Starting on your knees, get a full nelson by placing your arms underneath his arms and grasping your hands behind your opponent's neck as in photo 271. You may pin the man by shoving strongly with your left leg pressing down behind his neck and raising his left shoulder rolling him over until he is on his back. Since

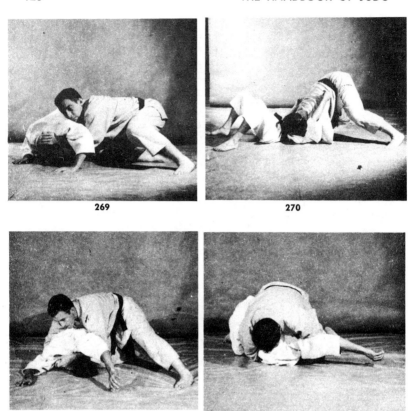

269                    270

271                    272

this hold uses pressure against the neck, it is illegal in competition.

## NEAR HALF-NELSON WITH ARM BAR

If your opponent is on his face, grab his right wrist with your right hand. At the same time, place your left arm underneath his left armpit, putting your hand on the back of his neck as in photo 273. Begin to lever your man on his back by lifting his left arm up and pressing down against the back of his neck, as in photo 274, until he is on his back, as in photo 275. You are still holding on to his right wrist with your right hand. His right arm is underneath his body, making it very difficult for him to move his right shoulder.

273  274

275  276

## NECK AND ARM LEVER

You attempt this technique when your opponent is lying flat on his stomach. Straddle your opponent and place your left arm underneath his left arm and shoulder. Place your right elbow on the back of your opponent's neck and grasp your hands together as in photo 276. Roll your opponent over, raising his left arm at the shoulder. Press strongly against the back of his neck with your right elbow keeping his right side snug against the mat as the left side raises, as in photo 277. As your opponent begins to roll over, step over his body, switching to his right side. Place his left arm against your left shoulder. Push with your feet and your left shoulder until your opponent is on his back as in photo 278.

277

278

## FAR-ARM DRAG

Wrap your arms underneath your opponent's body, grasping your hands above his right elbow. Place your chest against his left side as in photo 279. Pull his right arm and side down by pulling your arms close to your waist; at the same time raise his left side with your upper chest as in photo 280. Drive forward with your upper body, landing your chest against his as he finishes on his back.

279

280

### FAR-LEG DRAG

This technique is no more complicated than a football tackle. Place your arms around your opponent's legs down low. Place your left shoulder against his left hip. Place your right foot behind you as in photo 281. Snap your opponent on his back by pulling his legs and knees off the ground toward your stomach and right side. At the same time drive forward with your left shoulder until your opponent is on his back as in photo 282.

281

282

### FAR-ARM AND -LEG DRAG

This technique combines far arm drag and far leg drag. Place your left arm under your opponent's neck with your left hand on his right arm above his elbow. Your right arm wraps around his legs pulling his knees close to his forward body as in photo 283. Place your right shoulder snug against your opponent's left hip. For action, snap your arms toward you. Simultaneously, drive forward with your upper chest. Your opponent should spin on his back in mid-air as in photo 284. You may end up in a side pin if desired, as in Hold Down Techniques.

### CHIN TWIST

Facing your opponent on your knees, place your right arm under his neck and grip his chin firmly with your hand as in photo 285. Kick and straighten your left foot out to your right side, rolling onto your back and wrapping your right arm over the top of his

283

284

285

286

neck maintaining your grip on his chin as in photo 286. Continue
to roll, hitting your right knee against the mat. Roll your opponent
on his back by pulling his chin from his right to his left toward
his left shoulder. As his head turns to the left his body will be
forced to follow, causing him to roll on his back as in photo 287.
Continue to roll until you are on your stomach. You end up in a
smother pin as a modified upper four-corner hold or Kuzure Kami
Shiho Gatame. The chin twist is illegal in competition as are all
techniques that apply pressure to the vertebrae of the neck.

287

288

## BELT AND NECK OVER

Place your left hand on the back of your opponent's head and neck. Place your right arm between his legs and grasp his belt with your right hand. Pull your opponent close to you as in photo 288. Push down on the back of your opponent's head and neck with your left hand while you are lifting his crotch off the ground with your right arm (by lifting and pulling his belt). Straighten your right foot and drive forward as in photo 289. Continue to roll your opponent over. As you are doing so, let go of the belt with your right hand; wrap it around the back of his neck, grasp your left hand. Your right armpit should press into the back of your opponent's knee as in photo 290. Try to press your opponent's left knee to his forehead.

289

290

You end up in a modified upper four-corner hold as in photo 8 of Hold Down Techniques, although done on the opposite side. Learn to do your take downs and roll-overs on both sides with equal ease.

### SIDE-GRAPEVINE ROLL

When your opponent is on his hands and knees, quickly lie on your left side, place your left leg between his legs and wrap your left foot around his left ankle. Grab your opponent's right shoulder with your right hand as in photo 291. Straighten his left leg by straightening your left leg and pushing forward against his left ankle with your left foot. He will falter and roll toward his left side. Help him roll over your body by pulling him across with your right hand. Keep on rolling as in photo 292 until you are on top of your opponent as in Hold Down Techniques.

291                          292

### LEG AND ARM LIFT

When your opponent is on his knees, grab his left sleeve at the elbow with your left hand and grab his ankle with your right hand as in photo 293. Lift with both arms until your opponent is off the ground slightly, swinging his right side toward your feet as in photo 294. Drop to your knees pressing your chest against his. Wrap your right arm around your opponent's left leg and your left arm around his neck. Then grasp your hands. End up in an "overhead with far leg" hold as in Hold Down Techniques.

293                                    294

Note: I refer to an "overhead with far leg" hold against your opponent's left side, although the hold, as described in Hold Down Techniques, is demonstrated against the right side.

## SCISSORS AND ARM HOOK

When your opponent is on his hands and knees, place your left leg around his left arm. Pull it away from his body as in photo 295. Begin to roll over your left shoulder. Kick off with your right foot, scissor his arm with your left leg as in photo 296. Roll until your opponent's feet swing up into the air and his hips are resting against the side of your body. Grasp his right arm with both of yours and hug tightly as in photo 297.

Although photo 297 is not an osaekomi, if your opponent's head is bent forward and his arms are hooked, it is very difficult for him to get away. If desired, you may continue to roll until his shoulders touch the mat as in double bar arm of Hold Down Techniques, still hooking his arms and pressing his head forward. This again is an illegal hold in competition, but your opponent will find it very difficult to get out of in practice.

295

296

297

## SHORT RIB REST

Although this technique is illegal in competition, you can observe its effectiveness in practice. If your opponent is on his stomach, press the pointed part of your elbow against his right side between his belt and right shoulder blade as in photo 298. If done properly, the pain will be enough to force the man to roll quickly toward you and on his back to ease his pain as in photo 299. You can end up in an upward-arm crank as in Arm Lock Techniques.

## SHIN ON CALF

If your opponent is on his hands and knees, place your right shin and most of your weight on his left lower leg below his calf. Press down and toward you with your shin as in photo 300. Place your left arm under his right arm and wrap your arm behind his neck. Pull his hip toward you with your right hand as in photo 301. If done properly, the pain against his left leg will cause your opponent to roll on his left side to get away. Assist him to his back by levering his right arm up with your left arm and pressing his head forward as in photo 301. When he is on his back, press your chest against his and, holding his right sleeve with your left hand, switch into Kesa Gatame as demonstrated in Hold Down Techniques.

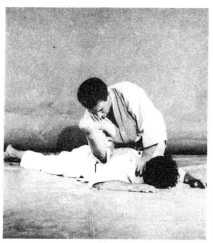

298

299

300                              301

CHAPTER **10**

# 'S' AS IN STRANGLE-SHIMEWAZA

BEFORE beginning any choke, be sure your hands are in proper position. The idea of choking is not to cut the wind, but to impede the blood flow to the head. Chokes are not dangerous if done properly. Do not practice chokes unless you are familiar with kwatsu, a special form of first aid and resuscitation, or a qualified instructor is present.

Chokes are useful outside the dojo if a man goes berserk or is a fighting drunk. When a man is drunk or goes mad, he won't feel the effect of a joint lock. You may break his arm in an attempt to subdue him and he will feel no pain. It is much easier to get behind him and choke him unconscious. Thus you can hold him until the proper authorities arrive. He should suffer no ill effects, providing he is in good health and providing you release the pressure as soon as he loses consciousness.

## PALMS UP

Relaxing your hands and arms, cross your arms, thumbs up, grabbing your opponent's collar behind his ears. Choke him by rolling your knuckles into his neck, turning your palms down. Pull him close to you. Spread your elbows. If possible, straighten his legs with your legs (photo 302).

302

303

## PALM UP, PALM DOWN

Reach your right hand in deep, palm down. Cross your arms. Your left hand is palm up. Hold a firm grip with your left hand. Start your choking by trying to touch your right elbow to your opponent's left shoulder (photo 303).

Note: Make sure both your arms are underneath your opponent's chin. Pull your opponent's upper body close to your chest and straighten his legs with your feet if possible.

## FRONT CROSSOVER, PUSH AND PULL

Grab your opponent's right lapel with your left hand, thumb up. Grab his left lapel with your right hand, thumb down, about six inches down from the neck. Cross over with your right hand as in photo 304. Push with your right hand and pull with your left.

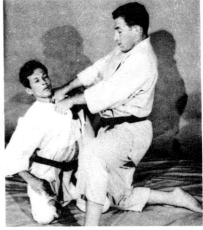

304

305

### HALF-BEAR CLAW

Your left hand holds your opponent's right lapel, thumb up. Your right hand holds high on his left collar, thumb down. Your right fist pushes in on the muscles of the left side of his neck while your left hand crosses over in front of his neck and pulls (photo 305).

### REAR DOUBLE-LAPEL TOURNIQUET

Hold your opponent's left collar with both hands. Slide your right hand up deep, then put your left hand on his right lapel as in photo 306. Your left hand holds his right lapel securely. With your right hand on his left collar, wind from left to right by straightening your elbow. Grapevine one or both legs around his if possible.

### REAR SINGLE-LAPEL TOURNIQUET

Grab your opponent's left collar with your right hand. Pull it across his neck tight. Then switch and hold it with your left hand, palm down. Put your right hand on his left shoulder as in photo 307. Choke your opponent by scissoring your forearms and spreading your elbows. Keep your wrists straight.

306                                          307

### REAR ONE-SIDE NAKED CHOKE

Wrap around his neck with your left arm, pointing your wrist toward the back of his collar as in photo 308. Using your right hand, slide your left forearm along the right side of his neck to the rear, pressing your left shoulder against the back of his head.

## REAR NAKED CHOKE

Place your left arm around your opponent's neck. Place your left palm on your right bicep with your right forearm in back of his neck, pushing forward. Squeeze both sides of his neck with your left arm. Push forward on the back of his neck with your right hand (photo 309).

308                                         309

## DOUBLE-BEAR CLAW

Place both hands on opposite collars, thumbs down below your opponent's ears. Your hands should be in very deep. Choke him, pressing your fists in his neck by straightening your arms at the elbows. Keep your wrists straight (photo 310).

## WINDING CHOKE

Grab your opponent's left lapel with your right hand and wrap it around his neck to his right. Your left hand should be under his left arm, behind his neck, and pushing forward. Choke by straightening both your elbows. Keep your right wrist straight. If at all possible while attempting this move, grapevine his left leg with your left leg. This will prevent him from rolling out of your choke (photo 311).

310

311

## HAND AND ELBOW, HOOKED ARMS

Your legs scissor your opponent's left arm. Your right arm hooks his right arm. This makes it very difficult for him to move his upper body. With your left hand, grab your opponent's left collar in deep. Push your elbow towards his neck on the right side as in photo 312.

## KNEE, FOREARM AND ELBOW

If your opponent has you in a side pin, reach your left hand over the back of his neck, grabbing your left pant leg at the knee. Keep a straight wrist and bend your elbow toward your left knee. Choke more strongly on his left side (photo 313).

312

313

### DOUBLE KNEE AND WINDING

This choke is not for competition. Place your opponent's head between your legs. Grab his right collar in deep. Pull across his neck and up as in photo 314. Place your left hand around your right wrist for more leverage.

Note: Keep your knees together so your opponent's head can not turn. In practice you may scissor your legs. This is illegal in competition.

### KNEE AND WINDING

Your opponent is on his back. The weight of your left knee is on your opponent's face. Hold his left lapel with both hands. Pull strongly as in photo 315. This move is illegal in competition.

314                              315

### DOUBLE KNUCKLE ROLL

Grip your opponent's collar, thumbs up. Choke by rolling your knuckles into his neck. At this point your thumbs should be pointing out. Your elbows should be close to your body and pressing forward. If you are attempting this choke on the ground, control your opponent's body with your feet (photo 316).

### WINDING AND ULNA PRESS

Your right hand grabs your opponent's left lapel in deep. Wind his collar around in front of his neck. Push the right side of his neck in a downward sliding motion with your left forearm. Grape-

316
317

vine a leg to prevent your opponent from rolling. This is a good counter to Seoi Nage—cross lapel throw (photo 317).

## COLLAR WINDING AND ROLL ON BACK

Grab your opponent's right collar with your right hand as in photo 318. Pull downward and begin your switch by kicking your left foot to your right and placing your right arm around your opponent's neck as in photo 319. The pressure of this choke is not to be put on until you are on your back. When you get on your back, your opponent is likely to attempt a pin as in photos 320 and 321. This will make it more difficult for him to get away. To complete your choke when on your back, grab your opponent's judo suit close to his neck on his left shoulder with your left hand and pull, elbows apart, sticking your chest out as in photo 321.

318
319

320                                    321

## Counters to Shimewaza or Strangling Holds

### LAPEL PULL

This counter works well against front crossover, push and pull chokes. Very simply grab both your lapels and pull them wide apart (photo 322).

### HAND ON FACE

This counter works well against Palm-up, Palm-down and others. When the man crosses his hands to choke you with his left hand on top, as in photo 323, slide your left hand under his left, over his right and on the left side of your face. This will cut down the tourniquet action of his hands, eliminating the choke.

322                                    323

(If, when he crosses hands, his right hand is on top; use your right hand.)

## FEET IN NECK AND HIP

A man may be trying any one of a dozen chokes. If you are on your back, place your left foot at his neck and your right foot at his hips. Using the mat as a wall, straighten your legs, pushing your opponent away (photo 324).

## HANDS PULL AND HUG

If your opponent is trying to execute a choke, preferably a cross-lapel variety, grab his hands and your collar and pull toward your waist (photo 325).

324

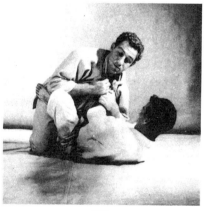

325

Note: Naturally, due to space limitations every counter cannot be shown, but here are just a couple of ideas of what you can do if a man grabs you from behind. Look at the rear single-lapel tourniquet (photo 6); you should duck your head slightly forward, strongly to your right side and try to come up facing your opponent by placing your head underneath his right arm thus unwinding his hands. Another way to counter a choke from behind: if a man tries a rear one-sided naked choke, as in photo 308, do an Ippon Seoi Nage or one-arm shoulder throw, as demonstrated in the te-waza or hand-throw section of the throwing techniques.

One thing very important to remember in choke counters is that if a man winds in for a choke, start to unwind before he has completed his technique, by switching or turning your body rapidly in the same direction he is trying to wind. If you roll or twist in the opposite direction he is trying to wind, it will aid him in his choke.

# CHAPTER 11

# GYAKUWAZA—THE ARMS HAVE IT

ARM lock techniques are safe if done with proper care. Do not jerk or yank on an arm lock. Put the pressure on gradually, allowing your opponent to submit before the arm is injured.

### DRAGGING ARM LOCK

After you have completed a throwing technique and your opponent is on his back in front of you, you are ready for your dragging arm lock. With both hands, hold your opponent's right wrist. His thumb should be pointing away from your body. Step your left foot over his head and snug into his neck as in photo 326. Lift his right shoulder by pulling upward on his wrist. Drag his wrist forward, stepping over with your right foot. In completing the dragging arm lock, you should be sitting on your opponent's right shoulder. His neck should be resting on your left calf as in photo 327. Raise your opponent's right arm at the wrist slightly, making sure his thumb is down.

326                  327

## STRAIGHT-ARM CRUSH

Start the same way for straight-arm crush as for dragging arm lock. Holding your opponent at the right wrist, step over with your left foot. Lift his right shoulder by raising his wrist. Lie down, keeping your body as close to your opponent's shoulder as possible, as in photo 328. With your opponent's thumb pointing upward and your knees close together, gradually arch your body, keeping your opponent's wrist pulled toward your upper chest.

328

### STRAIGHT-ARM CRUSH—Variation

You may start off from photo 326, stepping your left foot over and then your right. Pull your opponent's right arm upward. Sit on his shoulders. Fall backward, keeping your knees close together. Arch, sticking your stomach out and pulling his wrist toward your upper chest. Make sure your opponent's thumb is pointing upward as in photo 329.

**329**

### STRAIGHT-ARM HUG

Your right knee should be bent and pushing against the left side of your opponent's body. Your left leg is over your opponent's head and your foot is wrapped around his right arm as in photo 330. His left arm is extended and his wrist is resting on your neck. Put your right arm over your left, placing them above his elbow. Roll to your left, pulling your arms toward your belt. This will straighten your opponent's elbow, making him submit.

### STRAIGHT-ARM HUG—Variation

Put both knees into your opponent's body. His left wrist should be snug against the right side of your neck. Your palms should be above his elbow, pulling down and rotating to the left.

Note: Your opponent's neck is resting on your left shin. There is an empty space between his arm and your belt. Also note his left thumb should be pointing toward the mat (photo 331).

330

331

### REVERSE-ARM BAR

Your opponent is lying on his stomach. Your right armpit is resting on his left shoulder. Raise his arm at the wrist, putting pressure on his elbow and shoulder joint (photo 332).

### REVERSE-ARM BAR WITH FIGURE-4 SCISSORS

You place your left calf over your opponent's left shoulder. Your right knee is over your left ankle. Your right foot is between the mat and his chest. Begin to straighten your body. Push his wrist upward, keeping his thumb pointing down. The pressure is on his elbow (photo 333).

332

333

## REVERSE-ARM LOCK AND CROTCH DRAG

If your opponent is straight-arming you, turn from left to right, placing your left arm over his left arm and your left palm on the inside of his left thigh as in photo 334. Kick your left foot straight out and sit down. Raise your ópponent's left wrist with your right knee and hand. The pressure is on his elbow.

**334**                              **335**

## STEPOVER ARM DRAG

If a man continually pushes with his left hand in standing practice, this is an ideal time to attack with this technique. As your opponent makes a push with his extended left arm, lean slightly backward and place your right foot over your opponent's left shoulder. Pull his wrist toward your chest. You may go into a dragging arm lock as in photo 327 or straight-arm crush as in photo 328 from this move, or you may sit on his shoulder as in photo 337 until he hits the mat. You will be sitting on his shoulder and raising his wrist in a straight arm lock.

## ARM HUG

Rest your left knee on your opponent's neck and your right knee on his left side. Hug his arm (photo 338). Push your shoulder against his wrist. Place your hands below his elbow and pull your

336    337

hands toward your waist, sticking your stomach in and your chest out. The arm hug is the same as photo 331, only done from a different angle.

## SURFBOARD

This hold is self-explanatory. This is a good technique to hold a man in for a long period of time without strain to your body. The pressure is on his shoulders. This technique is not for competition (photo 339).

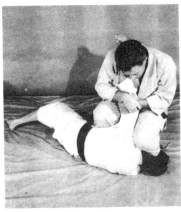

338    339

### FACING-STRAIGHT ARM LOCK

If your opponent grabs your belt in an attempt for a hip-style throw, quickly place your right forearm underneath his left elbow. Place your left arm on his left shoulder and your right palm on your left wrist. Straighten your arms, putting pressure on your opponent's elbow (photo 340).

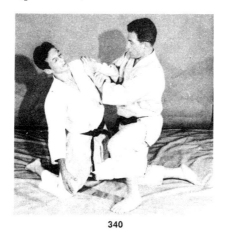

**340**

### DOUBLE STRAIGHT-ARM BAR

Place a leg over your opponent's shoulder and place your arms underneath his elbows. Raise up and stick your stomach out, pushing away with your leg. The pressure is on both of your opponent's elbows (photo 341).

**341**

### DOUBLE-ARM HUG

If your opponent is attempting to choke you without crossing his arms, place your left palm above his left elbow. Place your right palm at your left elbow. Pull away from your opponent and lean slightly forward. Pull his arms together at the elbows as in photo 342.

Note: If your opponent slips one of his arms out, you may switch over easily to a dragging arm lock.

### SINGLE-ARM HUG

If your opponent grabs your collar in an uchi mata (inside thigh sweep) attempt, wait until he pulls away from you, attempting to bend you over. This will straighten his arm. As he is pulling you down, join your hands above his elbow, rotating them to the left, pulling his arm close to your body as in photo 343.

Note: The rotation to the left straightens your opponent's arm, locking it. If you continue hugging the arm and bend forward at the waist, his head will go between your lower legs and, by falling on your back, you will end up in a straight-arm crush, with your right leg across his face.

342                              343

**DOUBLE-ARM HUG AND LEG HOLD**

This technique is illegal and should not be attempted in competition. If your opponent is lying on his back, step your right foot over his right foot and push his right ankle toward his belt as in

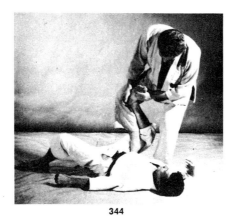

344

photo 344. Fall on your left side. Place your opponent's arms over his head by hoisting below his elbows as in photo 345. When his arms are straight, wrap your left arm around his left elbow and place your right hand on your left wrist. Lean to your left and pull your left shoulder in, squeezing both of his wrists against your neck and hug tightly at his elbows as in photo 346.

345

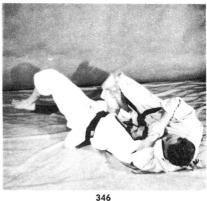

346

### SINGLE-ARM SQUEEZE

Lying on your back, extend your opponent's right arm close to your chest, and place your knees snug against his right shoulder. Grabbing his wrist, stretch and lock his arm away from his thumb to your left (photo 347).

347

## DOUBLE-ARM SQUEEZE

Lying on your back, place your knees below your opponent's elbows. Press in. Grab your opponent's wrists and pull outward away from his thumbs, putting pressure on his elbows (photo 348).

## LEG, NECK AND ARM LEVER

Lying on your back, place your opponent's head between your legs. Hook his right leg at the knee with your right leg. Place your left foot over your right.

Note: Your opponent's forehead and his right knee should be touching together. With his left arm straight and left thumb pointing down, push upward on his wrist. The pressure is against his shoulder (photo 349).

348

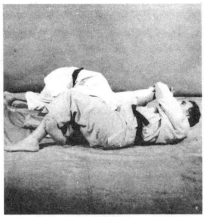

349

### STRAIGHT-ARM CRUSH—Variation

Lying on your back, pull your opponent's right arm close to your chest, straightening his arm. Place your right foot at his left shoulder, holding his body away. Place your left leg around his right arm shoving your foot under his chin (photo 350).

Note: Your left leg should wrap around your opponent's right arm above the elbow. With your left shin, push your opponent's neck up and back. Hold his wrist and push his arm in the opposite direction to his thumb, to your left. The pressure is on his elbow.

**350**

### SHORT-ARM SCISSOR

If your opponent bends his right arm, making you miss the straight-arm crush, place your left arm on the inside of his right arm as he is bending it. Help him by placing your right hand on his right wrist and shoving downward as in photo 351. Then place

**351**                                        **352**

your left leg over his right arm at the wrist. Hook your right leg over your left foot. Grasp your left hand with your right hand and straighten your left leg in order to press your opponent's right wrist towards his right shoulder. Arch your back and pull your hands toward your chest as in photo 352.

### WRIST LOCK AND HOLD DOWN

This technique is illegal in competition. In free practice or on the street, it is a good way to hold a man down for a long period of time without a great deal of effort. Place your right knee on your opponent's upper chest. Place your left knee on his chin. Flex your opponent's wrist, palm in, by grasping your hands around his hand and pulling toward your waist. In completing this technique, if your opponent refuses to bend his wrist, place your left knee and most of your weight on your opponent's face. This will distract his attention from his hand and the wrist will bend easily (photo 353).

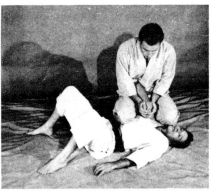

**353**

### FOREARM HAMMER LOCK

This hold is illegal in competition. Bend your opponent's right arm behind him. Place your left arm under his right wrist and place your left palm on your opponent's arm above the elbow. Raise your left arm and shoulder. With your right hand, grab either his collar, his hair or under his nose (photo 354).

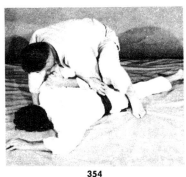 

354                 355

### FIGURE-4 HAMMER LOCK

This hold is illegal in competition. With your opponent lying face down, arm behind him, place your left foot between his right wrist and back and over his arm above the elbow. Hook your right leg around your left leg. With your right hand, grab your opponent's left shoulder. To apply pressure, push your stomach forward and upward toward his head, keeping your left knee bent. The pressure is on his shoulder and elbow (photo 355).

### UPWARD ARM CRANK

Place the weight of your chest on your opponent's chest. Grab your opponent's right wrist with your right hand. Place your left hand under his right upper arm and over your right wrist, grabbing your wrist securely as in photo 356. Pull his wrist downward toward his waist, raising his elbow slightly.

### REVERSE TIME HOLD

Hold your opponent in a smother pin or modified upper four-corner hold as in Hold Downs. Hold your opponent's right arm close to your chest and around your waist. Swing your legs forward alongside his and switch on to your back quickly. His arm should still be around your chest, only now it is reversed and bent across your waist. Place your left foot over his body. To apply pressure, arch your back, pushing your stomach up, raising his right elbow and lowering his wrist. The pressure is on his shoulder (photo 357).

356

357

## TIME HOLD

With your left hand, put your opponent's right upper arm over your right leg. Then place your right lower leg on top of your opponent's right wrist. Hook your left leg around your right ankle. Place your right arm around your opponent's head and grip with your left hand. To apply pressure, pull your opponent's head upward, force your stomach forward and straighten your left leg. This will bend your opponent's arm backward over his right shoulder as in photo 358, putting pressure on his right elbow and right shoulder.

358

## DOWNWARD ARM CRANK

In the previous three photos, the arm was cranked upward. The next two photos show the arm cranking downward. Place the weight of your chest on your opponent's chest. Grasp his right wrist with your left hand. Place your right hand under his right arm and over your left wrist. To apply pressure, pull his wrist toward his shoulder, raising his elbow slightly. The pressure is on your opponent's shoulder (photo 359).

359          360

## ELBOW LIFT AND SHOULDER LOCK

Start off with Kesa Gatame. Grab your opponent's right sleeve with your left hand. Your right arm is around his head. Switch your right hand to your opponent's right elbow. To apply pressure, stick your chest out, raise your opponent's right elbow, lowering his wrist, and turning to the left slightly (photo 360).

Note: The ideal time to attempt this technique is when you have your opponent in side pin, scarf hold, or Kesa Gatame. In trying to escape, your opponent grasps your belt with his right hand and pushes you away, slightly raising his right shoulder off the mat. Then switch into your technique. If you find that you cannot apply the amount of pressure you want, scoot closer to his shoulder and head.

### FRONT ELBOW CRANK

The pressure of this technique is on the elbow and the muscles two inches on either side of the inside of the elbow joint. Straddling your opponent, raise your body slightly, giving your opponent an opportunity to roll. As he rolls to his right, wrap your left arm around your opponent's left arm jamming your left wrist hard into his left elbow. Place your left elbow snug against your left hip making it difficult for him to slip his hand out. Grab your left hand with your right hand and place your right foot on the mat. Lean toward his left front as in photo 361. Then lift your left knee off the ground, cross it over his body, straightening your left leg. At the same time, bend his elbow from the weight of your upper body and the momentum of your left leg swinging across his body. Your left elbow touches the mat. You try to touch his left wrist to his left shoulder with pressure from your armpit as in photo 362.

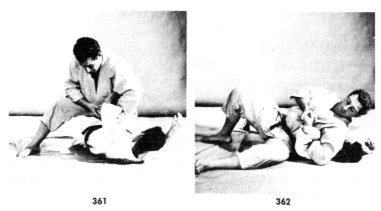

361    362

### REVERSE ELBOW CRANK

The pressure of this technique is much the same—on your opponent's elbow and the muscles two inches on either side of the inside of his elbow. If you are trying an upper four-corner hold and smother, as in Hold Down Techniques, don't put your full weight on your opponent's chest. Give him a chance to roll. As he begins to roll to his left, raising his right shoulder, wrap your left arm around his right arm, placing your left wrist at his left elbow. Grab your left hand with your right and place your right foot flat on the mat as in photo 363. Place your left arm close to your left side so his right arm and wrist will not slip away. Place your weight on your right leg, swinging your left leg through until you are in a sitting position. Your left elbow should be touching the mat and your right hand still grabs your left hand firmly. For pressure, lean backward, scooting your hips forward, pressing your left armpit and shoulder on his right wrist, forcing it toward his right shoulder as in photo 364.

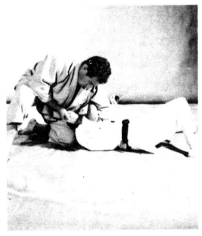

363

364

CHAPTER **12**

# 'NECKING' NOT ALLOWED— NONCOMPETITIVE NECK LOCKS

## NECK CRANK AND SIT OUT

IF your opponent is behind you trying to grab your legs, fall forward onto your face. If he is holding on to your legs, he will also fall onto his face. Scoot back again quickly, hooking both legs under his arms, shoving his head between your legs and pressing your weight on the back of his head as in photo 365. Keep your hands close together and begin to roll by pulling back strongly with your left leg as in photo 366. Strain until you are in a sitting position and your opponent is on his back as in photo 367.

You may go into this another way by holding your opponent in a smother pin. If his arms raise over his head in an attempt to grab your legs, put your legs over his arms; shove his head between your legs and rise to a sitting position.

Note: To put pressure on, lean forward, pushing your stomach forward. The pressure is on your opponent's neck.

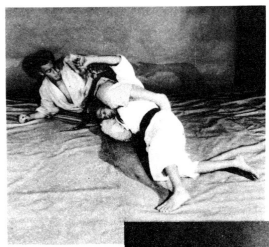

365

366

367

## REVERSE STOCKS AND SIT OUT

First get your opponent in Kesa Gatame or scarf hold (See Hold Downs). Let your opponent try to get out by letting him begin to sit up. Hold tight with your right hand as before. Let go with your left arm and swing it around in back of your opponent's neck and under his right arm. Scoot forward and lean back as in photos 368 and 369. The pressure is on your opponent's neck.

368                                              369

## FORWARD NECK CRANK

Place the back of your opponent's head against your lower abdomen. Wrap your hands around one of his legs. Lean forward, pushing your opponent's chin to his chest. The pressure is on his neck (photo 370).

370

### FORWARD NECK CRANK—Variation

This technique is much the same as photo 367, neck crank and sit out. You are in a sitting position as in photo 367, but the difference is that you shove your opponent's head to your left, placing his head between your left thigh and left side. Grab your opponent's leg, bending his head forward. You may put pressure on his neck by leaning forward. If desired, you may roll onto your back and hold the same technique (photo 371).

371

### REVERSE FIGURE-4 NECK LOCK

Place your right hand on your opponent's left shoulder. Wrap your left arm under your opponent's neck and on top of your right wrist. Press your chest against the back of his neck. Slide your left arm to your right across his neck, lifting your left elbow close to your chest. You are choking the right side of your opponent's neck while putting pressure on it (photo 372).

372

## REAR FACE AND NECK LOCK

From behind, grab your opponent's neck with your right palm up and left palm down. Place your left forearm below your opponent's left ear. Pull your arms close to your body. Lean forward, bending his head downward. The pressure is on your opponent's neck and chin (photo 373).

**373**

## FORWARD FIGURE-4 NECK LOCK

Lie on your opponent's stomach. Double-grapevine his legs. Place your right arm underneath the back of his neck, placing your right hand on your left bicep. For pressure, place your right shoulder under your opponent's chin and push with it toward the top of his head. Squeeze your right arm into the back of his neck. Lift your left elbow toward your waist (photo 374).

**374**

## FRONT FACE LOCK

Wrap your left arm around your opponent's neck below his ear. Grasp your right hand. The left side of your opponent's head is against your stomach. For pressure on the neck and face, step forward, lowering your waist slightly, and rear backward (photo 375).

375

## FRONT NECK CRANK

Sit on your opponent's stomach. Pin his shoulders with your knees. Pull your opponent's head forward toward your right thigh (photo 376).

376

## Illegal Pressure Holds

### CHIN LIFT

Place your left knee in the small of your opponent's back. Place your hands under his chin, turning his head slightly to the right. Rear back slowly (photo 377).

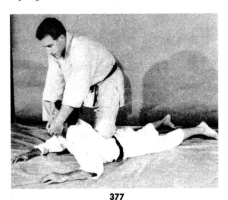

377

### ARM-HEAD PUSH

Grapevine your opponent's left leg with your left leg to prevent his rolling to his right side. Push his left arm across and in front of his face. Grab his left wrist with your right hand from behind his head. Place your left hand against his head and push. Pull toward your chest with your right hand. The pressure is on his left shoulder and neck (photo 378).

378

## SPINE STRETCH

If your opponent is on his hands and knees, double-grapevine him from behind. Put your chest against his back, hook your arms around his face, straighten his legs by straightening yours, and arch your back. Pull his head away from the mat toward your chest while continuing to arch your back. The pressure is against his spine (photo 379).

**379**

## ABDOMINAL STRETCH

Grapevine your opponent's left leg with your left leg to prevent his rolling to the right. Slide your upper body underneath his right arm. Wrap your hands around his neck. Pull your hands close to your chest. Straighten your body, pushing your stomach forward. The pressure is on his abdominal muscles (photo 380).

**380**

# CHAPTER 13

# LOCKING THE LEGS

LEG locks are illegal in judo competition because the leg muscles are so strong that you are unsure of the actual pressure being applied. Thus, your leg could easily be broken before you decide to submit.

### KNEE LOCK

Place your leg between your opponent's legs, spreading his feet. Grab his right pant leg or his right ankle on the inside as in photo 381. Leaving your left foot in place, bend over, grasping his pant

381

382

leg at the knee with your left hand while putting his left foot under your right armpit. Step over to his right side with your right foot as in photo 382. Turn your right knee to the left and lean your upper body to the right, putting pressure on your opponent's knee.

### HALF-CRAB

Start with your opponent on his back. Grab his left ankle in the crook of your left arm, pulling and lifting his left leg close to your body. Step across his body with your right foot, keeping your left foot in place, turning him onto his stomach. Still keeping his left leg snug against your body, bend at the knees and lean back slowly (photo 383).

383

384

### BOSTON CRAB

Start with your opponent on his back. Grab a leg under each of your armpits. Hold tightly at the ankles. Step across his body with one foot keeping your pivot foot in place, making him roll onto his stomach. Bend your knees and lean back slowly. The pressure is on the small of his back (photo 384).

### STEP-OVER KNEE LEVER

With your opponent lying face downward, place your left ankle behind and against his left knee. Your left knee should touch the mat on the outside of his leg and the toes of your left foot should touch on the inside of his leg. Lift his foot up. Your right knee touches the mat between your opponent's legs. Your left ankle should be in the bend of your right knee. His left foot is against your stomach. To apply pressure, grab your opponent's belt with your right hand and lean forward (photo 385).

385

## OVER SCISSORS

If the man gets you in a scissor grip around the stomach, turn your back to him. If his left foot is on top of his right, put your right ankle on top of his left ankle. Place your left leg over your right ankle and arch your back, as in photo 386. Remember to put your opposite leg over the leg he has on top when you are doing an over scissors.

386

### REVERSE DOUBLE FRONT GRAPEVINE LOCK

Place your knees on the mat on the inside of your opponent's legs. Hook your ankles around his ankles. Put the palms of your hands on the inside of his knees. Push his knees outward and down. Attempt this technique when your opponent is on his back and you are on top of him and he wraps his leg around the outside of your legs, as in photo 387.

**387**

### DOUBLE FRONT GRAPEVINE LOCK

With your opponent on his back, wrap your legs around the outside of his thighs and hook your feet on the inside of his ankles. To put pressure on, straighten your legs, raising his body. You may add pressure by spreading your legs and his legs slightly (photo 388).

**388**

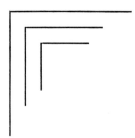

# GLOSSARY

AGO: chin
AKA: red (as in "Red & White" teams)
ASHIKUBI: ankle
ASHIWAZA: leg throws
ATAMA: head
ATEMIWAZA: striking techniques
BUTSUKARI: body contact or bump
CHIISAI: small
CHIKARA: power; using one's strength
DAN: grade
DE: advance
DO: waist or trunk
DOJIME: squeezing opponent's abdomen with legs
DOJO: place of judo practice; gymnasium
ERI: collar
FUKEI: parent's association
FUSENSHO: win by default
GYAKU: reverse to lock a joint
HADAKA: naked, without jacket (as in a choke)
HAJIME: first; referee's command to "Begin the match"
HANE: spring or jump
HANSOKUMAKE: loss by violation of rules
HANTAI: opposite or reverse

HANTEI: decision in match
HARA: stomach
HARAI: sweep
HIDARI: left
HIJI: elbow
HIKIWAKE: draw; tie; even
HIZA: knee
IPPON: one point (Ippon wins a match)
ITAMI-GATCHI: winner; opponent can't continue
ITAMI-WAKE: draw by injury
JIGOTAI: defensive posture
JIKAN: referee call for "time"
JUJI: cross
JUDO: gentle way; body-contact sport
JUDOGI: loose-fitting, strongly woven cotton jacket; loose-fitting
    cotton trousers and cotton belt (no buttons or zippers)
JUDOKA: judo participant
JUJITSU: forerunner of judo; a means of killing or seriously injur-
    ing one's opponent
KACHI: win
KAESHI: counter
KAKE: the action necessary to complete a throw
KANSETSUWAZA: arm-lock techniques; joints
KAO: face
KATA: prearranged exercises demonstrating judo principles
KATAKA: one half
KATAI: hard; stiff
KATAME: grappling
KATSU: to win
KEIKO: practice
KIAI: an offensive shout in a match; a shout or grunt putting all
    of one's strength in one movement. If done right, you may startle
    your opponent. For example, if somebody behind you blows a
    whistle loud, honks a car horn or screams in your ear and you
    are not expecting the onrush of loud noise, you usually straighten
    your body and stiffen up just for a split second. In competition,
    if you startle your opponent and make him stiff for a second when
    you attack with your technique, the man should go over like
    a stiff wooden board. To counter any technique, you must be
    relaxed. Note also that in competition if you use kiai while
    attempting a technique, it is considered good judo.

KOSHIWAZA: hip throw

KUBI: neck

KUMIKATA: methods of holding

KUZUSHI: to break an opponent's balance

KYU: brown belts and lower (class)

MAITTA: shout in a match meaning "I give up"

MAKE: to lose

MIGI: right

MOMO: thigh

MOROTE: both arms

MUNE: chest

NAGEWAZA: throwing techniques

NEWAZA: mat work or grappling techniques (also known as katamewaza)

O: major or great (as in *O goshi,* hip throw, or *O uchi gari,* inner reaping throw)

OBI: belt

OKII: big, large

OSAEKOMI: hold down or referee's call on holding thirty seconds for win

OSAEKOMI-TOKETA: referee's call that hold is broken and time should stop

OSU: push

OTOSHI: drop down

RANDORI: free practice, not contesting

REI: greeting or salutation (done by bowing)

RENZOKUWAZA: combination technique

SENSEI: teacher

SHIAI: contest

SHIHAN: term of high respect for teacher, usually reserved for Dr. Jigora Kano, founder of Kodokan judo.

SHIMEWAZA: choking techniques of strangling against the neck

SHIMPAN: referee or umpire

SHIRO: white

SHIZENTAI: natural standing posture

SHIZENTAL, JIGOTAI: natural defensive posture

SHOBU: contest

SODE: sleeve

SONO-MAMA: referee's call to "stop" or "freeze"

SORE-MADE: referee's call, "That's all" or "Match is over"

SOTO: outer

SUKOSHI: little
SUKUI: scoop up
SUTEMI: self-sacrifice to throw opponent by throwing yourself
SUTEMIWAZA: back and side throws
TACHIWAZA: throws from standing position (also known as Nage-waza)
TAI: body
TAISABAKI: body movements in judo
TAISO: calisthenics
TATAMI: sectional straw mat. Preferred mat for judo contesting
TATE: vertical
TE: hand
TEKUBI: wrist
TEWAZA: hand throws
TOBI-KOMI: skip in
TOMOE: circular
TSUKURI: to attain the necessary position before executing a throw
TSURI: pull and lift in circular motion similar to a hook
TSUYOI: strong
UCHI: inside
UCHIKOMI: practicing position of any techniques for form. Usually repeated many times in order to perfect a movement or hold
UDE: arm
UKEMI: break falls or falling exercises
URA: counter
USHIRO: back
UYE: up
WAZA: technique
WAZAARI: referee's call of "half-point"
WAZAARI; AWASETE-IPPON: referee's call meaning, one-half point, and one-half point together score one point, or the match
YAWARAKAI: soft
YOKO: side
YUBI: fingers
YUDANSHA: one holding the rank of black belt
YUDANSHAKAI: an association of black-belt holders
YUSEIGACHI: to win a contest by a decision
ZAREI: bowing from a kneeling position

# Index